Chord Chemis SONGBOOK

This publication is not authorised for sale in the United States of America and/or Canada.

Wise Publications
London / New York / Sydney / Paris / Copenhagen / Madrid / Tokyo

Exclusive distributors:

Music Sales Limited
8/9 Frith Street, London W1D 3JB, England.

Music Sales Pty Limited
120 Rothschild Avenue Rosebery, NSW 2018,
Australia.

Order No.AM952930
ISBN 0-7119-8188-4
This book © Copyright 2000 by Wise Publications

Unauthorised reproduction of any part of
this publication by any means including
photocopying is an infringement of copyright.

Written and arranged by Arthur Dick
Book layout and music processing by Digital Music Art
Photography by George Taylor
Edited by Sorcha Armstrong
Cover design by Michael Bell Design
Front cover photographs courtesy of Rex Features
and London Features International

Printed in the United Kingdom by
Printwise (Haverhill) Limited, Haverhill, Suffolk.

Your Guarantee of Quality
As publishers, we strive to produce every book to
the highest commercial standards.
The music has been freshly engraved and the book has
been carefully designed to minimise awkward page turns
and to make playing from it a real pleasure.
Particular care has been given to specifying
acid-free, neutral-sized paper made from pulps which have
not been elemental chlorine bleached.
This pulp is from farmed sustainable forests and was
produced with special regard for the environment.
Throughout, the printing and binding have been planned
to ensure a sturdy, attractive publication which should
give years of enjoyment.
If your copy fails to meet our high standards,
please inform us and we will gladly replace it.

Music Sales' complete catalogue describes
thousands of titles and is available in full colour
sections by subject, direct from Music Sales Limited.
Please state your areas of interest and send a
cheque/postal order for £1.50 for postage to:
Music Sales Limited, Newmarket Road,
Bury St. Edmunds, Suffolk IP33 3YB.

www.musicsales.com

Welcome to the Chord Chemistry SONGBOOK

This book is intended as a companion to the **Chord Chemistry** tutor book (*see page 48 for more details*). It can be used together with the tutor book to help you learn exciting new chords, or simply as an easy way to learn some of your favourite songs.

All of the songs featured in this book have been chosen because they illustrate the chord types and voicings that are introduced in the tutor book - so for each song you'll find a **CHORD CHECK** reference indicating which page to look at in *Chord Chemistry* to find more information.

Each song has been specially arranged to follow the style of **Chord Chemistry**, with lyrics, chords and rhythm slashes. Chord shapes are illustrated with photographs throughout, and alternative shapes and voicings are given wherever appropriate.

The **Chord Chemistry** system is the exciting new way to transform your basic chord skills into professional-sounding guitar parts!

Contents

A Design For Life - Manic Street Preachers 14

The Fool On The Hill - The Beatles 20

Happy Xmas (War Is Over) - John Lennon 6

Hey Joe - Jimi Hendrix 4

How Deep Is Your Love - The Bee Gees 26

Hush - Kula Shaker 34

I Can See For Miles - The Who 37

I Got You (I Feel Good) - James Brown 40

I Shot The Sheriff - Bob Marley 24

If I Ever Lose My Faith In You - Sting 44

Michelle - The Beatles 32

Papa's Got A Brand New Bag (Pt.1) - James Brown 22

Paranoid - Black Sabbath 42

Sgt. Pepper's Lonely Hearts Club Band - The Beatles 8

Tears In Heaven - Eric Clapton 30

T-Shirt Suntan - Stereophonics 11

While My Guitar Gently Weeps - The Beatles 28

Wonderwall - Oasis 17

Hey Joe

Basic Chord Shapes

> **CHORD CHECK**
>
> See *Chord Chemistry* pages 7-8.

This Hendrix classic was released in December 1966, as the first single from *The Jimi Hendrix Experience*. Although not written by Jimi, it launched the 'Underground Rock' scene at the time, this version being much slower and heavier than the original (which had been a hit for The Leaves in the U.S.). The sequence of five chords cycles throughout the song's verses and solos, and with Jimi's sound and touch, just blows you away!

Here are the five chords in sequence:

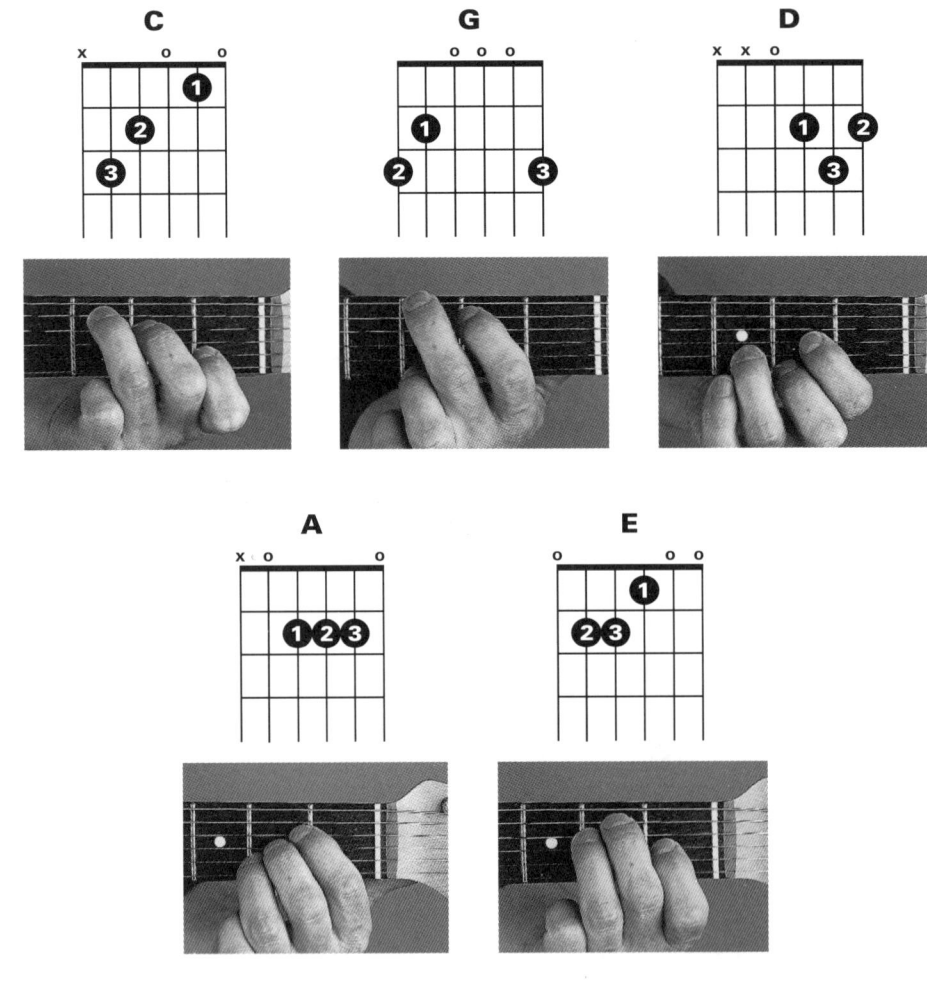

THE BIG LIVE SOUND...

Jimi's huge sound, generated by all those Marshall amplifiers, was difficult for the mikes of that time to record - be warned!

 **TIP**

Here are some alternative fingerings for you to try.

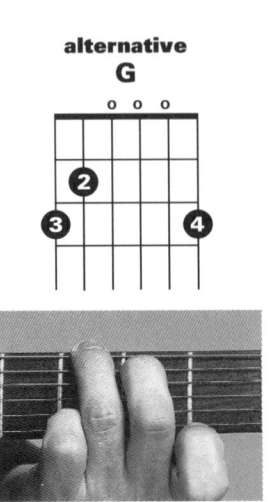

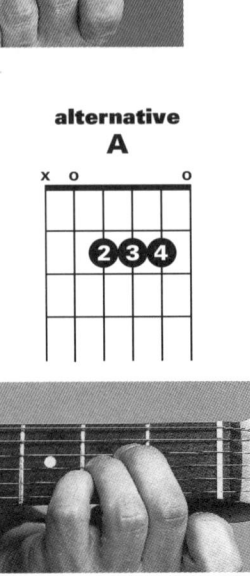

4 CHORD CHEMISTRY SONGBOOK

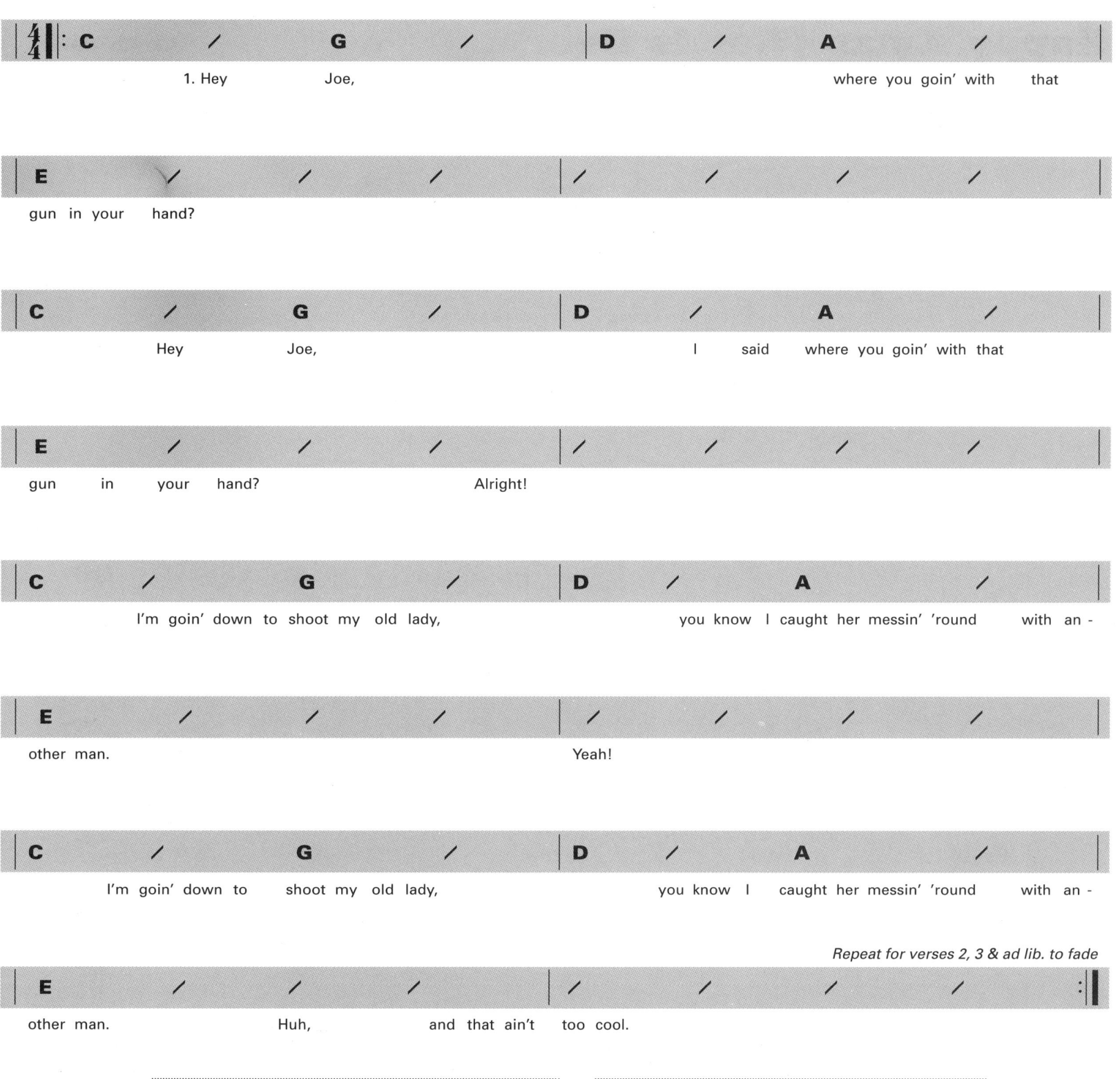

VERSE 2

Hey Joe, I heard you shot your
Woman down, you shot her down now
Hey Joe, I heard you shot your old
Lady down, you shot her down in the ground
Yes I did, I shot her
You know I caught her messin' round
Messin' round town
Uh, yes I did, I shot her, you know I
Caught my old lady messin' 'round town
And I gave her the gun, I shot her!

VERSE 3

Hey Joe, said now, uh, where you gonna run
To now, where you gonna run to? Yeah
Hey Joe, I said, where you gonna run to now,
Where you, where you gonna go?
I'm goin' way down south, way down to
Mexico way, alright!
I'm goin' way down south, way down where
I can be free, ain't no one gonna find me babe!
Ain't no hangmen gonna, he ain't gonna
Put a rope around me!
Hey Joe... *(etc. ad lib. to fade)*

Words & Music by William M. Roberts
© Copyright 1962 Third Story Music Company Incorporated, USA.
Carlin Music Corporation, Iron Bridge House, 3 Bridge Approach, London NW1 for the British Commonwealth
(excluding Canada and Australasia) and The Republic of Ireland.
All Rights Reserved. International Copyright Secured.

Happy Xmas (War Is Over)

Using The Sus 2 And Sus 4

CHORD CHECK
See *Chord Chemistry* pages 12-14.

John Lennon's famous anti-war anthem provides a great workout for the **sus** and **add** shapes you learnt in *Chord Chemistry*. See page 4 for the basic chord shapes **E** and **D**.

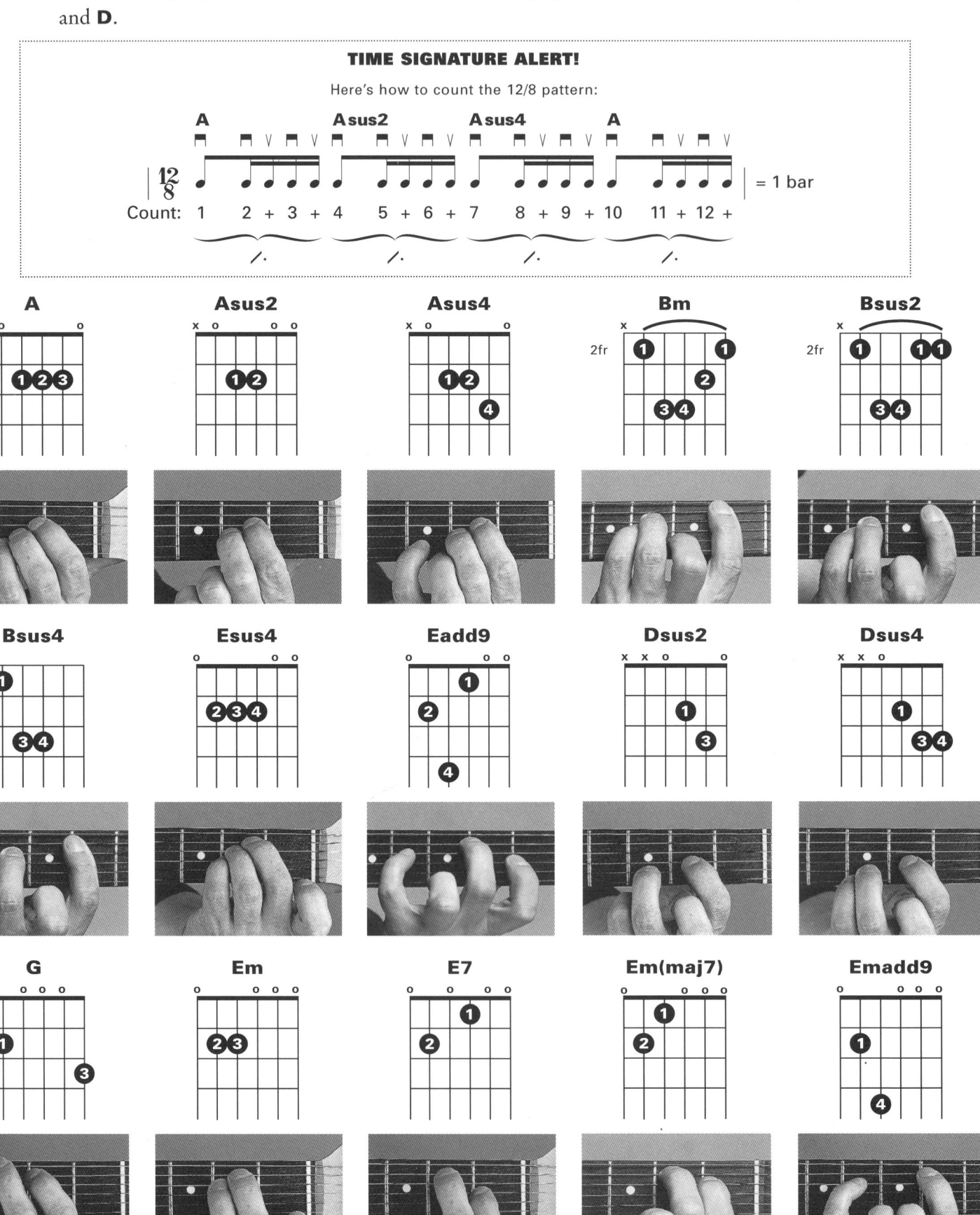

12/8

Verse

| ‖: A | Asus2 | Asus4 | A | Bm | Bsus2 | Bsus4 | Bm |

1. So this is Xmas and what have you done? Another year

| Esus4 | E | Eadd9 | E | A | Asus2 | Asus4 | A |

over, a new one just be-gun. And so this is

| D | Dsus2 | Dsus4 | D | Em | Em(maj7) | Emadd9 | Em |

Xmas, I hope you have fun the near and the

Chorus

| Asus4 | A | Asus2 | A | D | Dsus2 | Dsus4 | D |

dear ones, the old and the young. A very merry

| G | ∕· | ∕· | ∕· | A | ∕· | ∕· | ∕· |

Xmas and a happy New Year, let's hope it's a

Repeat for verses 2 & 3

| Em | ∕· | G | ∕· | D | ∕· | E7 | ∕· :‖

good one, without any fear. And so this is

| ‖: A | Asus2 | Asus4 | A | Bm | Bsus2 | Bsus4 | Bm |

War is ov - er if you want it,

Repeat to fade

| Esus4 | E | Eadd9 | E | A | Asus2 | Asus4 | A :‖

war is ov - er now.

VERSE 2

And so this is Xmas, for weak and for strong
The rich and the poor ones, the road is so long
And so happy Xmas, for black and for white
For the yellow and red ones, let's stop all the fights.
A very merry Xmas *(etc)*

VERSE 3

And so this is Xmas, and what have we done?
Another year over, a new one just begun
And so this is Xmas, I hope you have fun
The near and the dear ones, the old and the young.
A very merry Xmas *(etc)*

Words & Music by John Lennon & Yoko Ono
© Copyright 1971 Lenono Music/Ono Music.
All Rights Reserved. International Copyright Secured.

Sgt. Pepper's Lonely Hearts Club Band

Introducing The Dominant 7th

CHORD CHECK
See *Chord Chemistry* page 20.

D.I. BOX
The guitars were recorded either from an amp or a fuzz box 'direct injected' into the recording console – a revolutionary technique in its day.

The title track from what is considered one of The Beatles' greatest albums is a perfect track to show off your 7ths. The three guitars on the original recording share the lead and rhythm by each playing the chords in different positions and with different sounds.

One of the rhythm guitars could play these open chords:

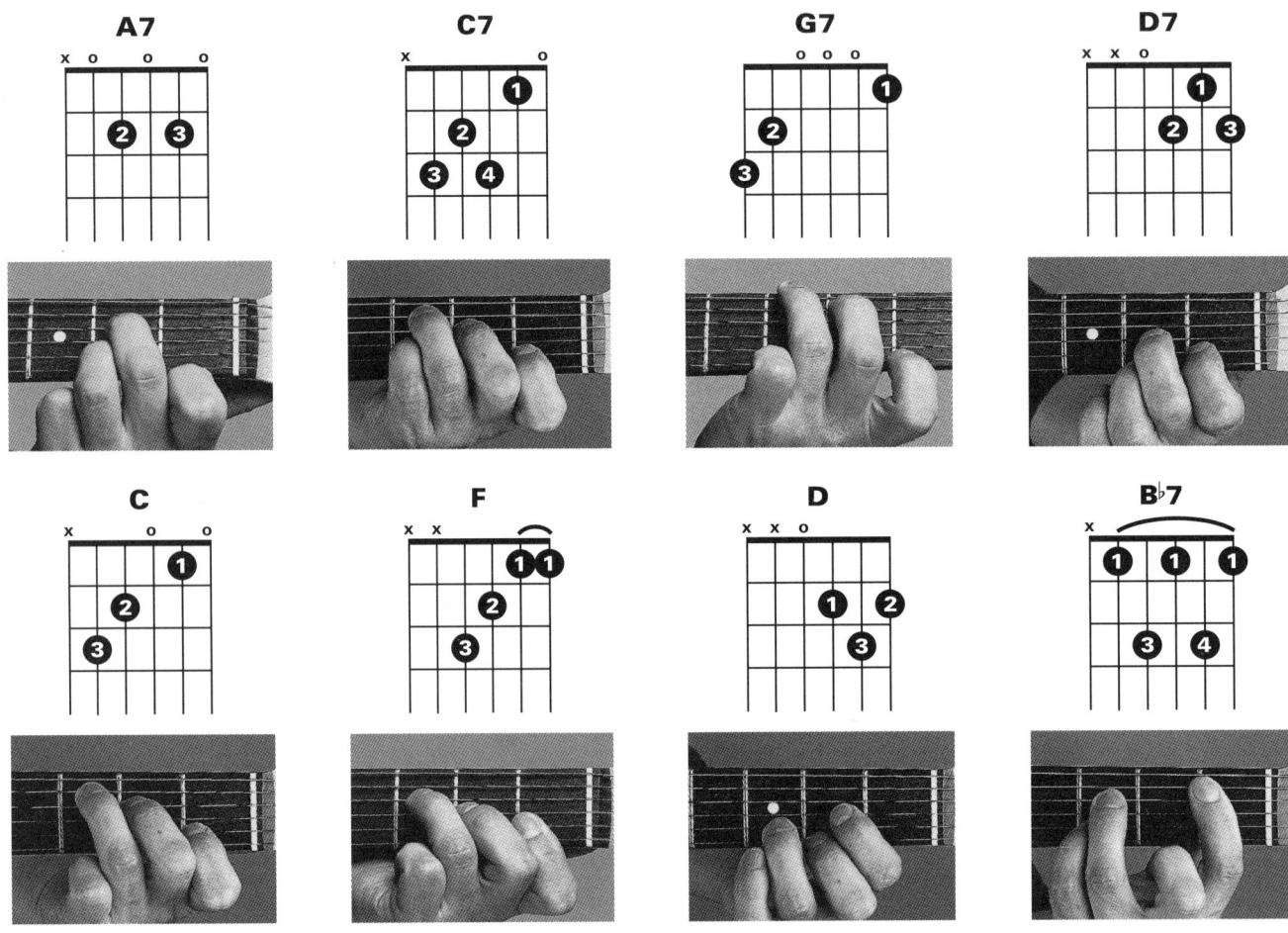

As an alternative, try using some moveable chords – see *Chord Chemistry* page 41.
Experiment with mixing the various types, The Beatles did!

TIP
No need to play all six strings.

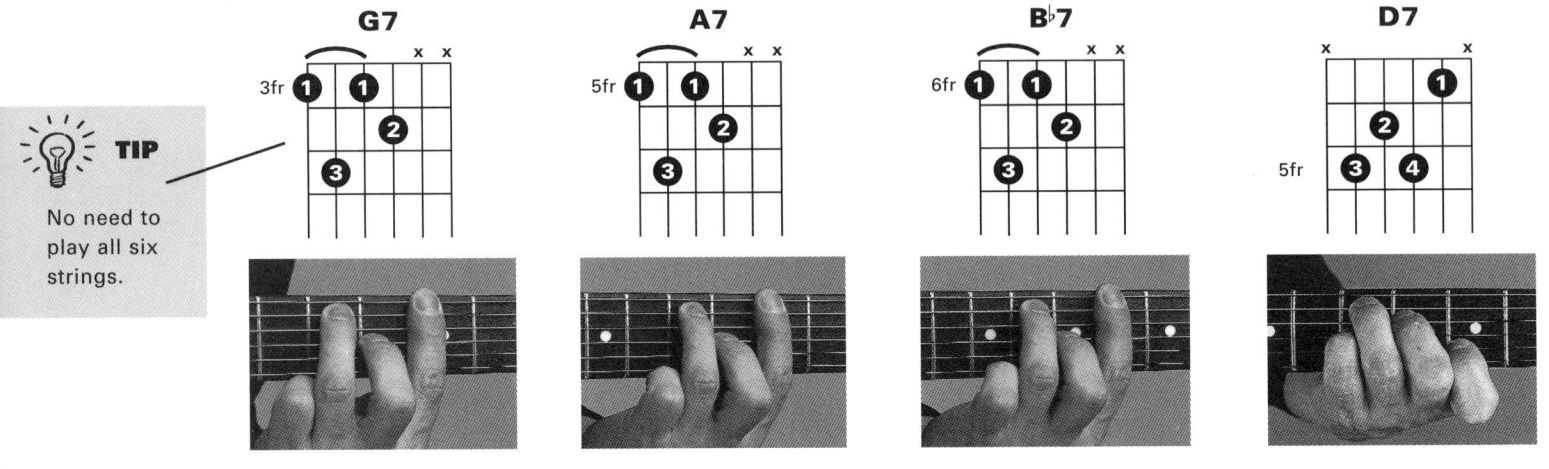

8   CHORD CHEMISTRY SONGBOOK

Intro

| **4/4** A7 / / / | / / / / | C7 / / / | G7 / D7 / ‖

1. It was

Verse

| G7 / A7 / | C7 / G7 / |

twenty years a-go today, Sergeant Pepper taught the band to play. They've been

| G7 / A7 / | C7 / G7 / ‖

going in and out of style, but they're guaranteed to raise a smile. So

| A7 / / / | C7 / / / ‖

may I intro-duce to you the act you've known for all these years,

| G7 / C7 / | G7 / / / ‖

Sergeant Pepper's Lonely Hearts Club Band.

Interlude

| C / / / | F / / / | C / / / |

| D / / / | D7 / / / ‖

We're

Chorus

| G7 / B♭7 / | C7 / G7 / |

Sergeant Pepper's Lone - ly Hearts Club Band, we

| C7 / / / | G7 / / / ‖

hope you will en-joy the show.

| G7 / B♭7 / | C7 / G7 / |

Sergeant Pepper's Lone - ly Hearts Club Band, sit

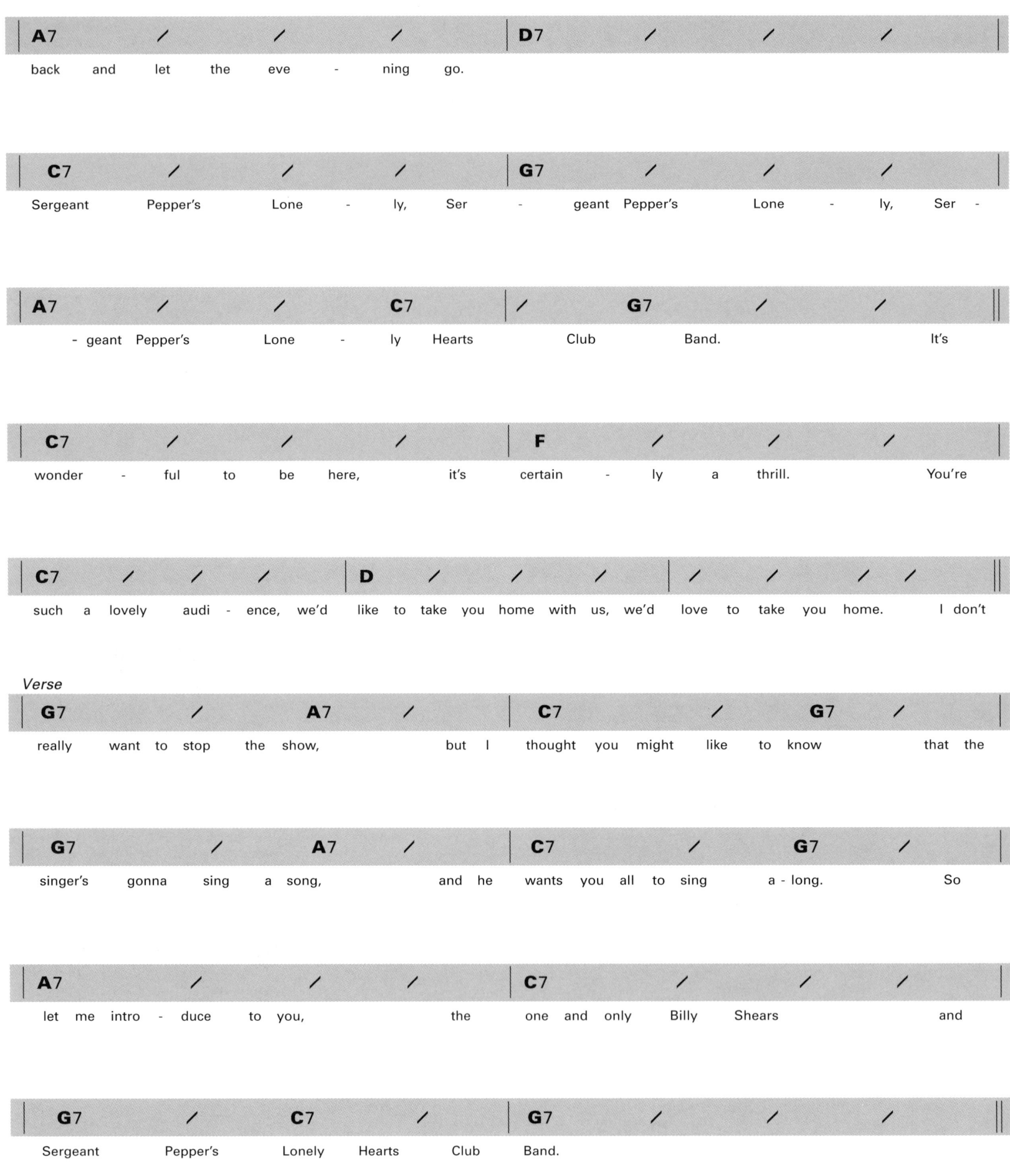

T-Shirt Suntan

The Add 9 & Sus 4

CHORD CHECK

See *Chord Chemistry* pages 10, 11 & 14.

The opening (and closing) four bars of **Aadd9** in this Stereophonics classic are played arpeggio fashion, i.e. single notes at a time. The guitars play a driving rhythm throughout, except for the bridge where they cool off a little.

VERSE PATTERN

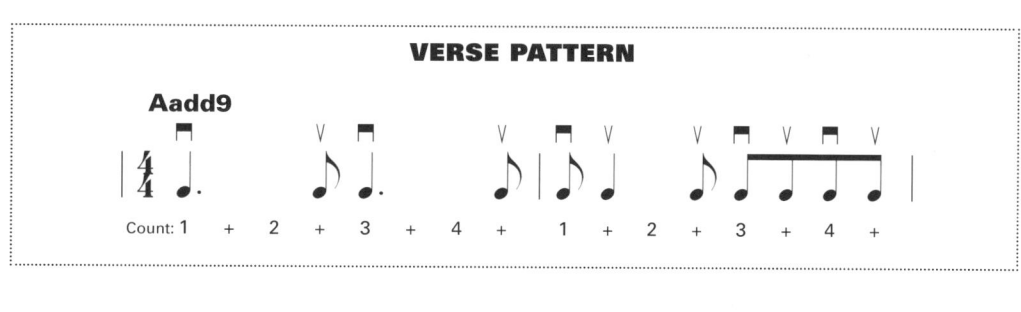

TIP

Compare this version to the 2nd fret position Aadd9 (See *Chord Chemistry* page 10) – this one comes from the Fadd9 version, moved up four frets!

Aadd9

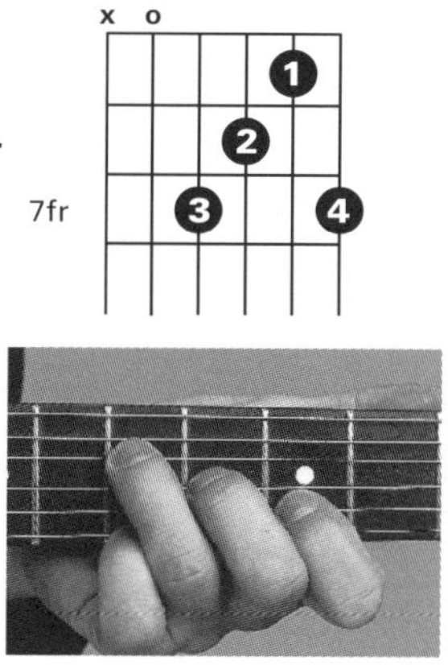

C♯m7

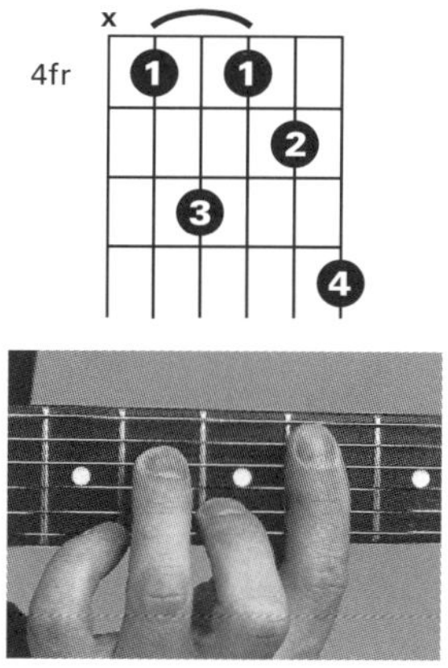

D

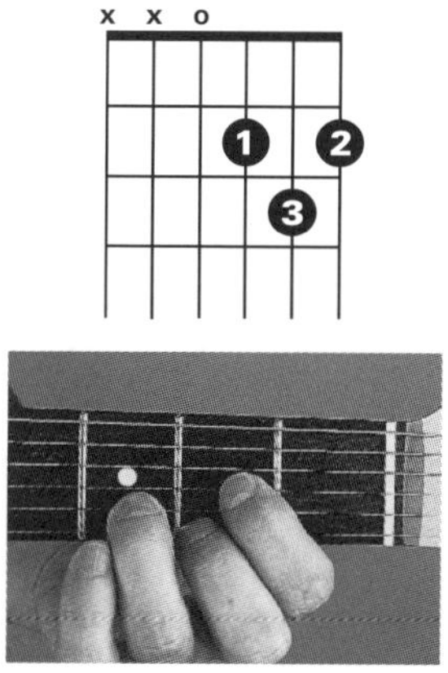

Dm

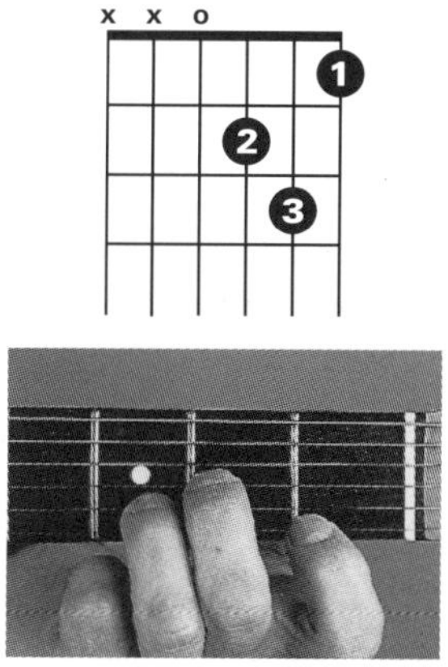

E7

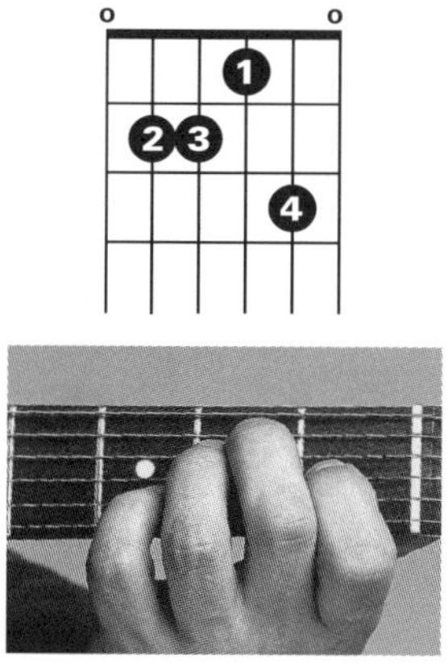

G5

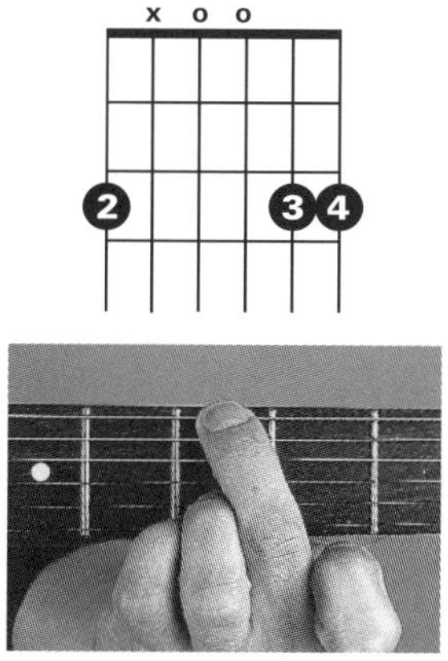

C5

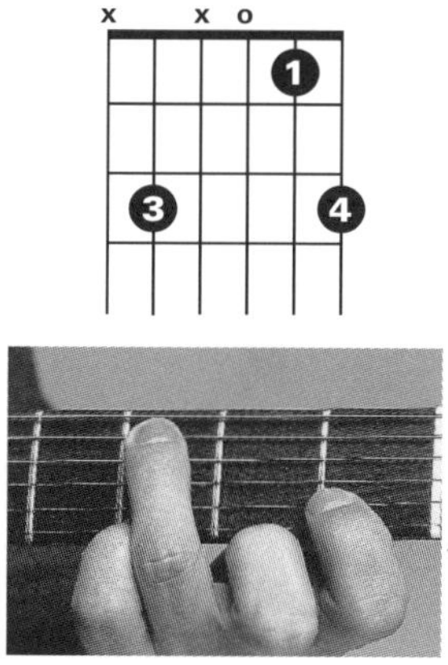

Fadd9

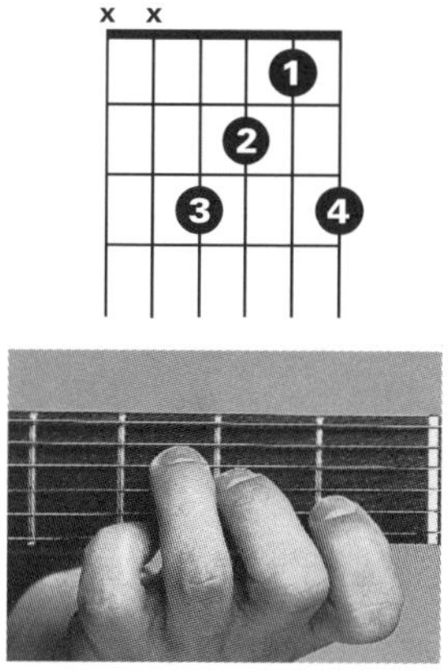

Am7

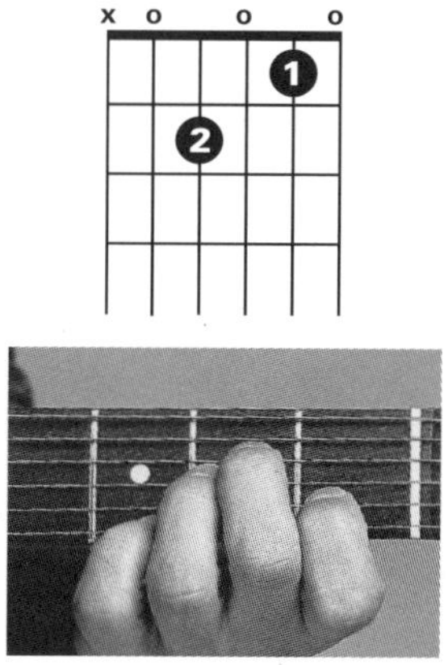

B♭sus2

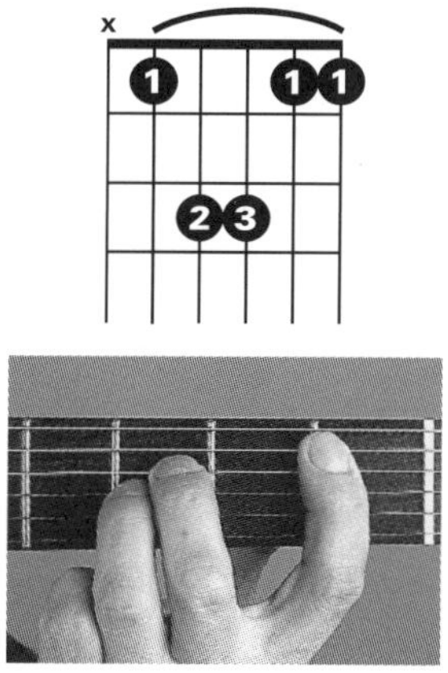

F

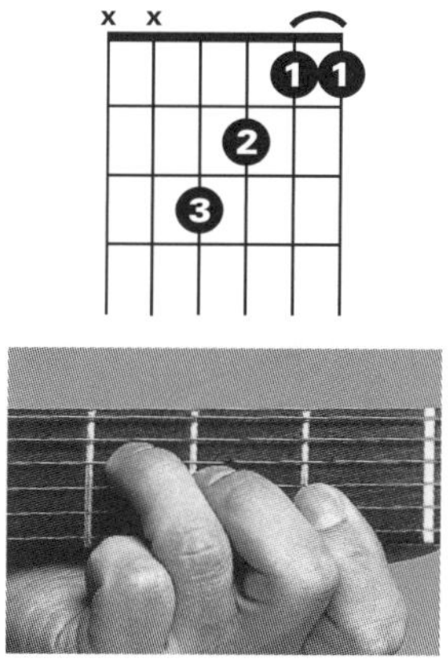

Fsus2

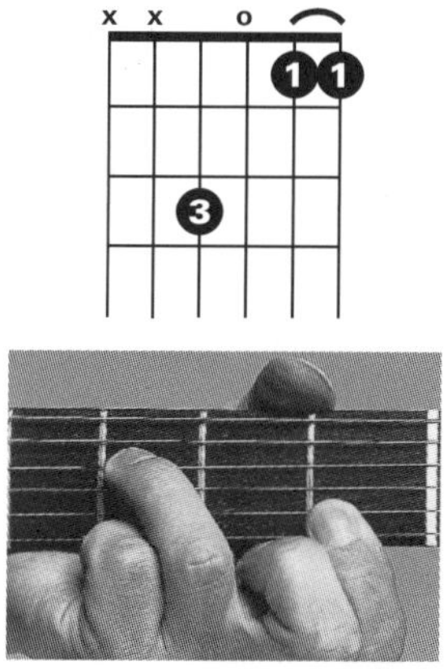

Em7

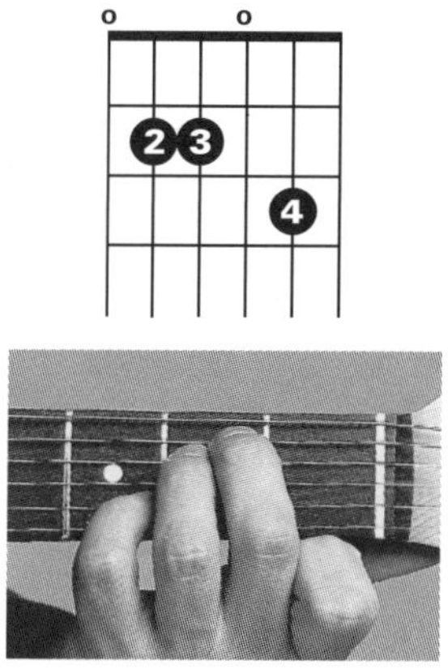

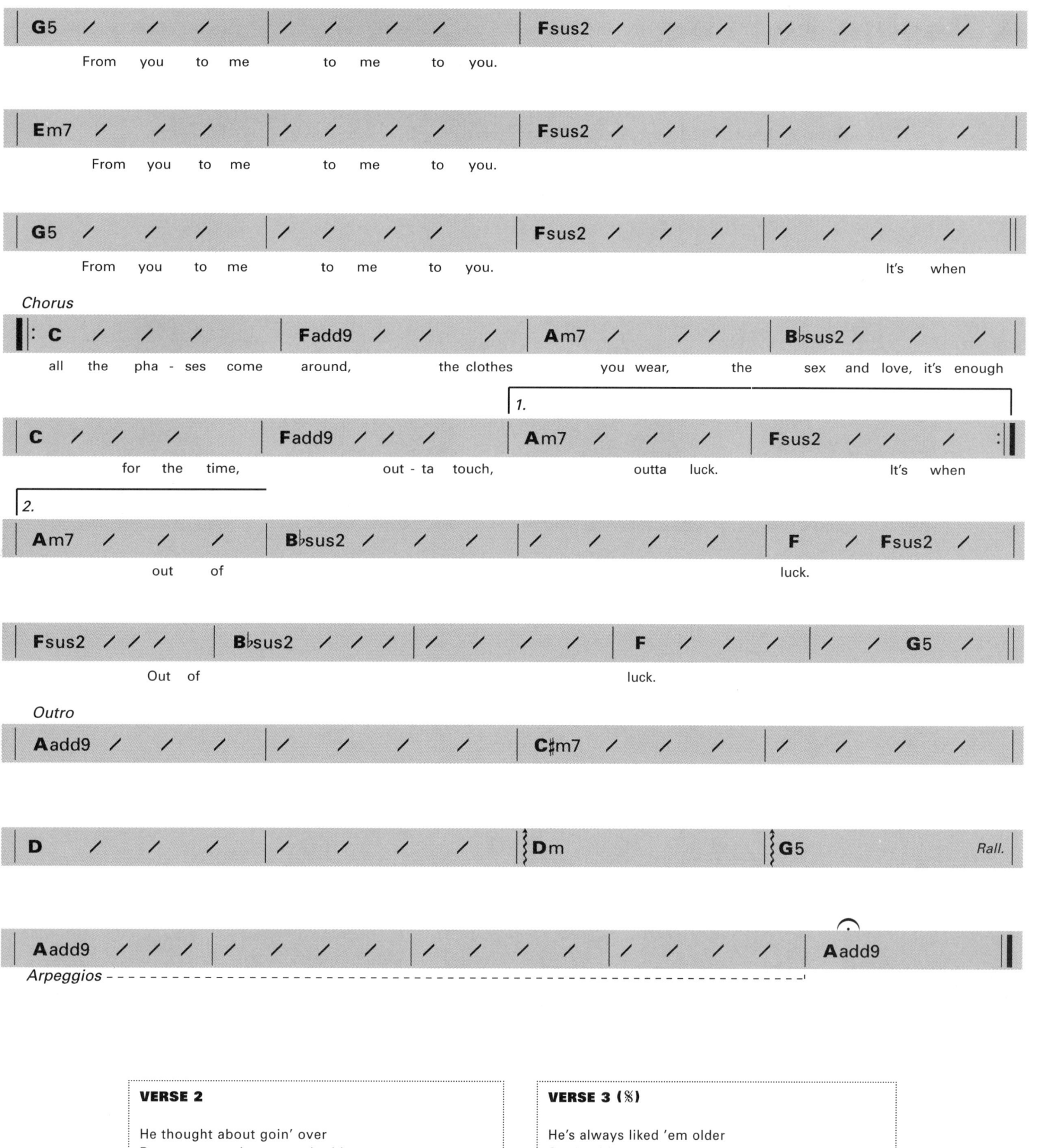

VERSE 2

He thought about goin' over
But you were always much older
And your sex dressed breasts impressed too.
He'd really like her to get it together
Before the twelfth of never
So he's comin' over.

VERSE 3 (𝄋)

He's always liked 'em older
So that his top lip touched on her shoulder
Lionized, undisguised, kill for you.
Like to show you his t-shirt suntan
Like to show you his minute headstand
Then a gun spun open.

Words by Kelly Jones. Music by Kelly Jones, Richard Jones & Stuart Cable
© Copyright 1998 Stereophonics Music Limited/Universal Music Publishing Limited, 77 Fulham Palace Road, London W6.
All Rights Reserved. International Copyright Secured.

A Design For Life

Using The Major 7th

The **major 7** chords that feature in this Manic Street Preachers song can be played using the basic shapes you learned in *Chord Chemistry*. However, we've also shown James Dean Bradfield's own chord voicings, which fit the sequence perfectly!

> **CHORD CHECK**
> See *Chord Chemistry* pages 18 and 19.

Compare: **Cmaj7** to **Cmaj7** and **E♭maj7** to **E♭maj7**

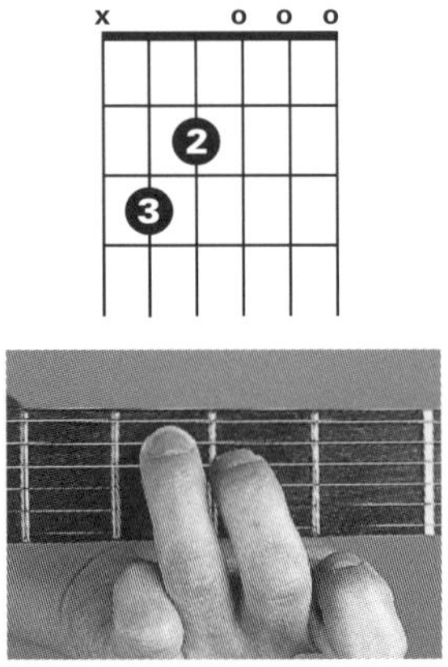

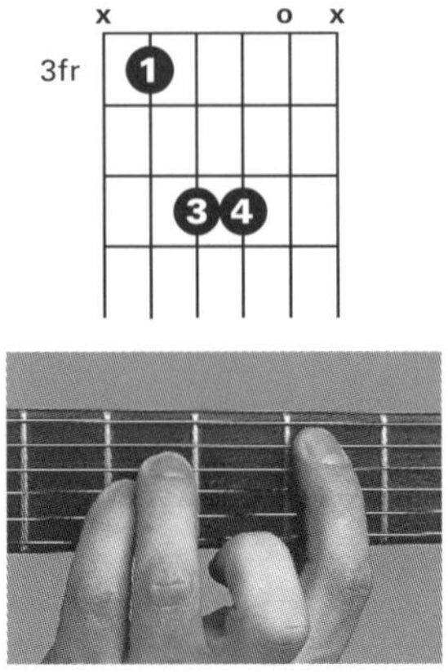

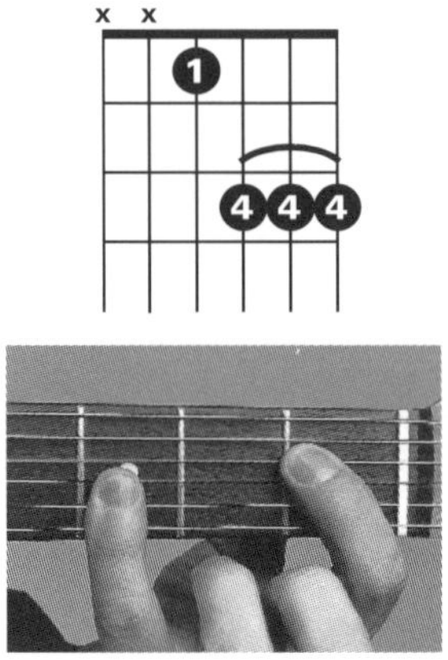

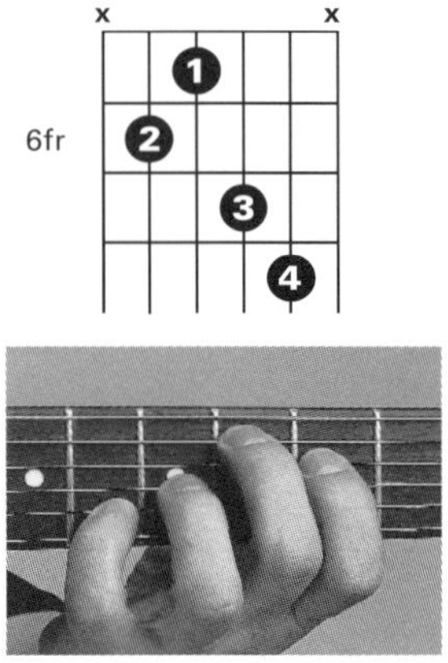

The verses and choruses in 'A Design For Life' should be played in an arpeggio fashion throughout:

Cmaj7 = 1 bar

Count: 1 2 3 4 5 6 7 8 9 10 11 12

Time indicator: /. /. /. /.

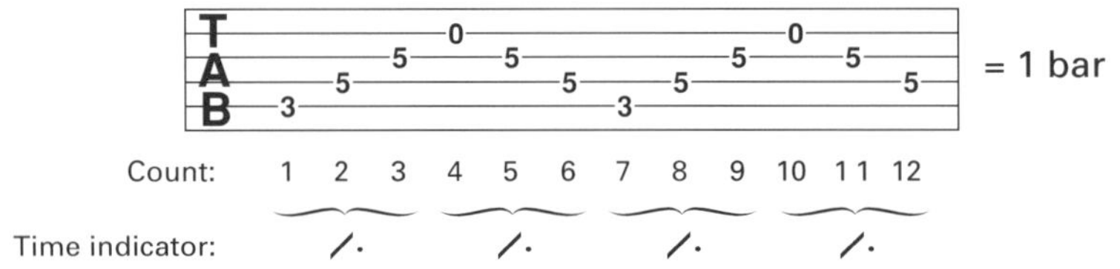

Dm7/6 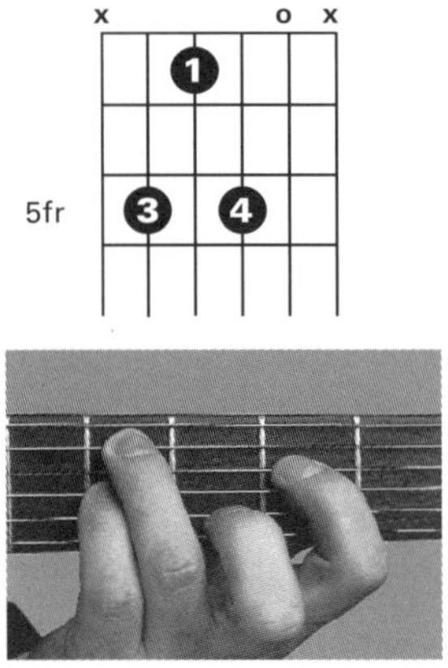   **G7** 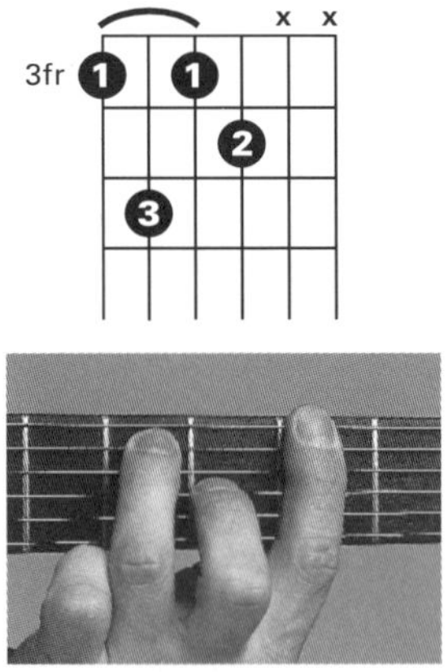   **Dm7♭5** 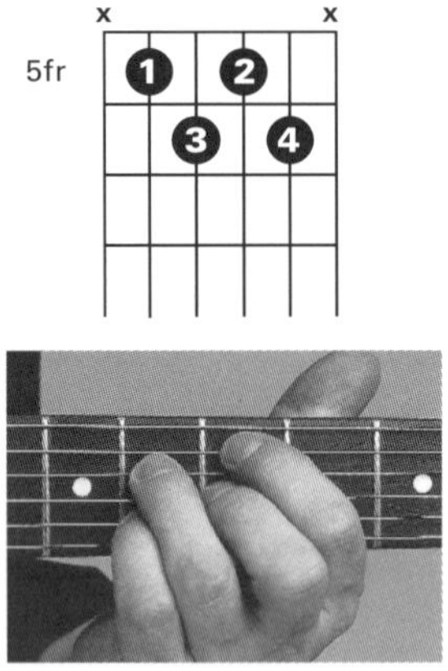   **Dm** 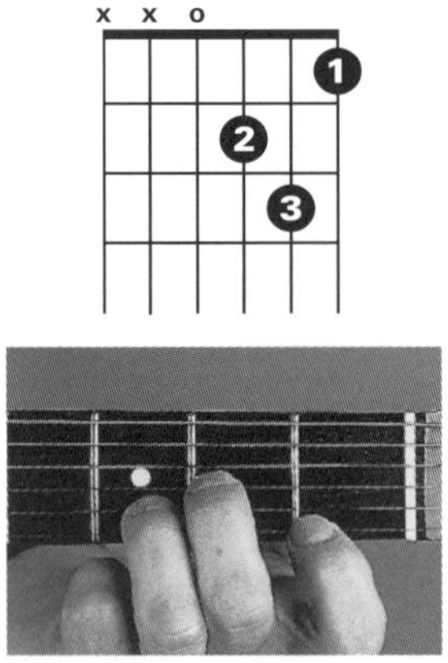   **G5**

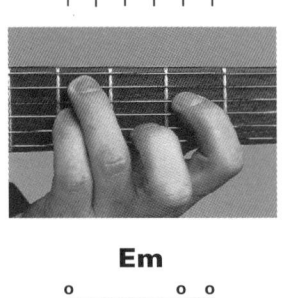
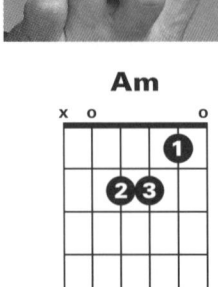

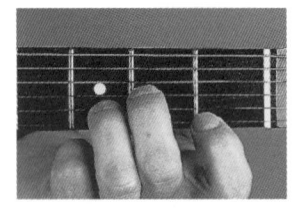

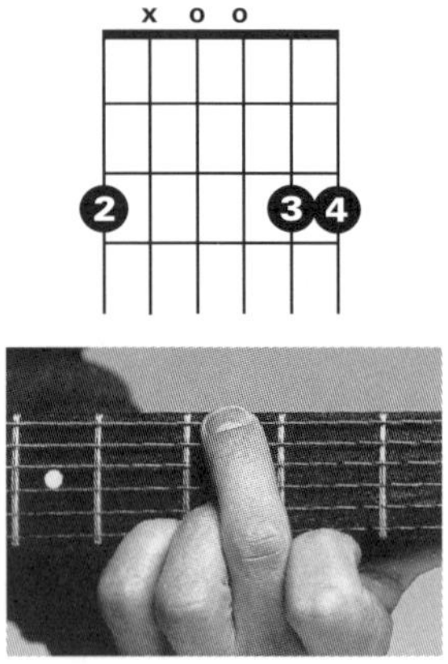

Em   **Am**   **Am7**   **Fsus2**   **F5**

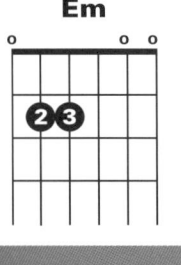
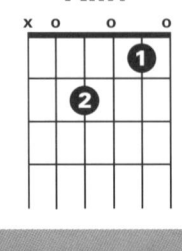
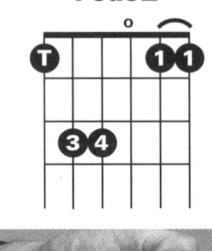
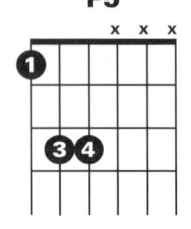

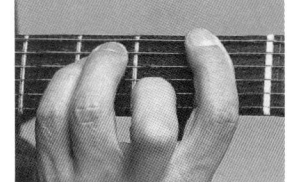

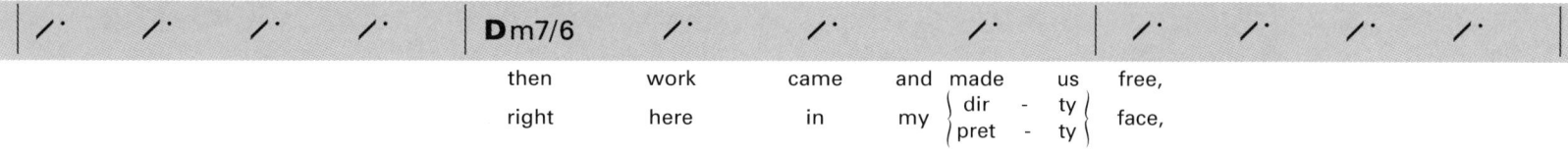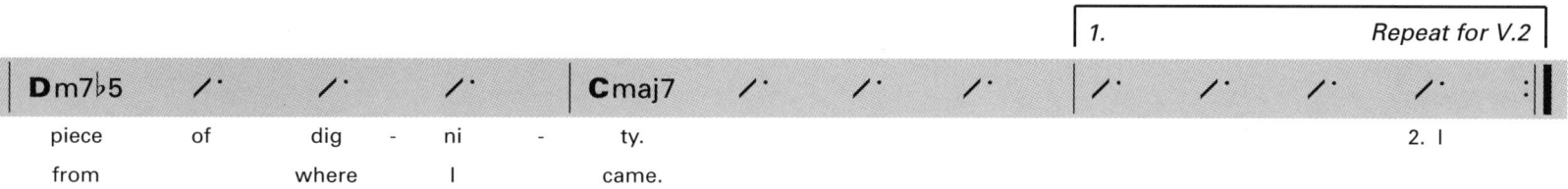

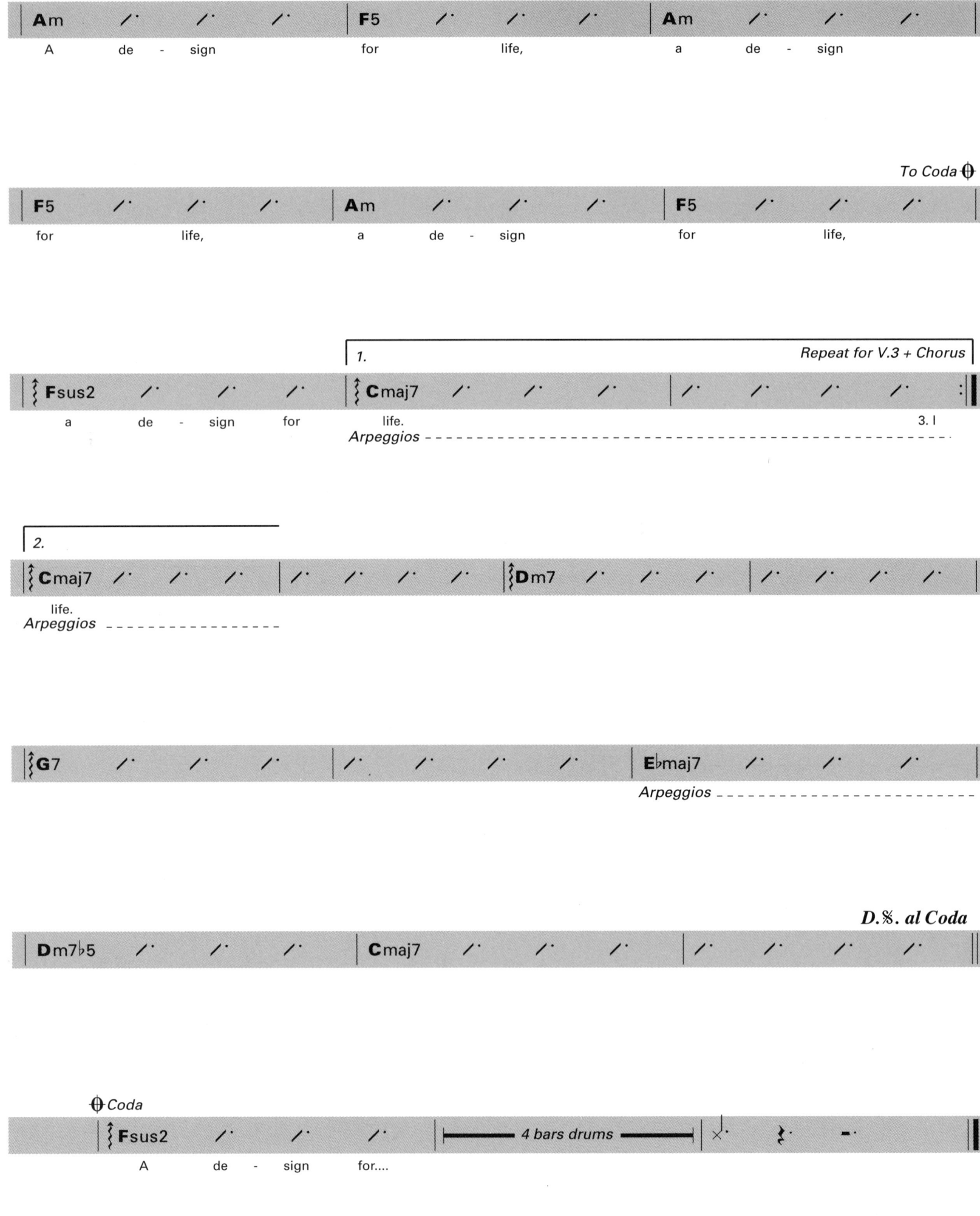

Wonderwall

Let It Ring...

This sweeping rock anthem from the second Oasis album *(What's The Story) Morning Glory?* is the classic example of a progression where most of the chords share common tones – in this case the D and G on the top two strings. The chord boxes that are shown here are in normal (non-capo-ed) positions, but to play along with the song you'll need to use a capo at the second fret.

> **CHORD CHECK**
> See *Chord Chemistry* pages 38-40.

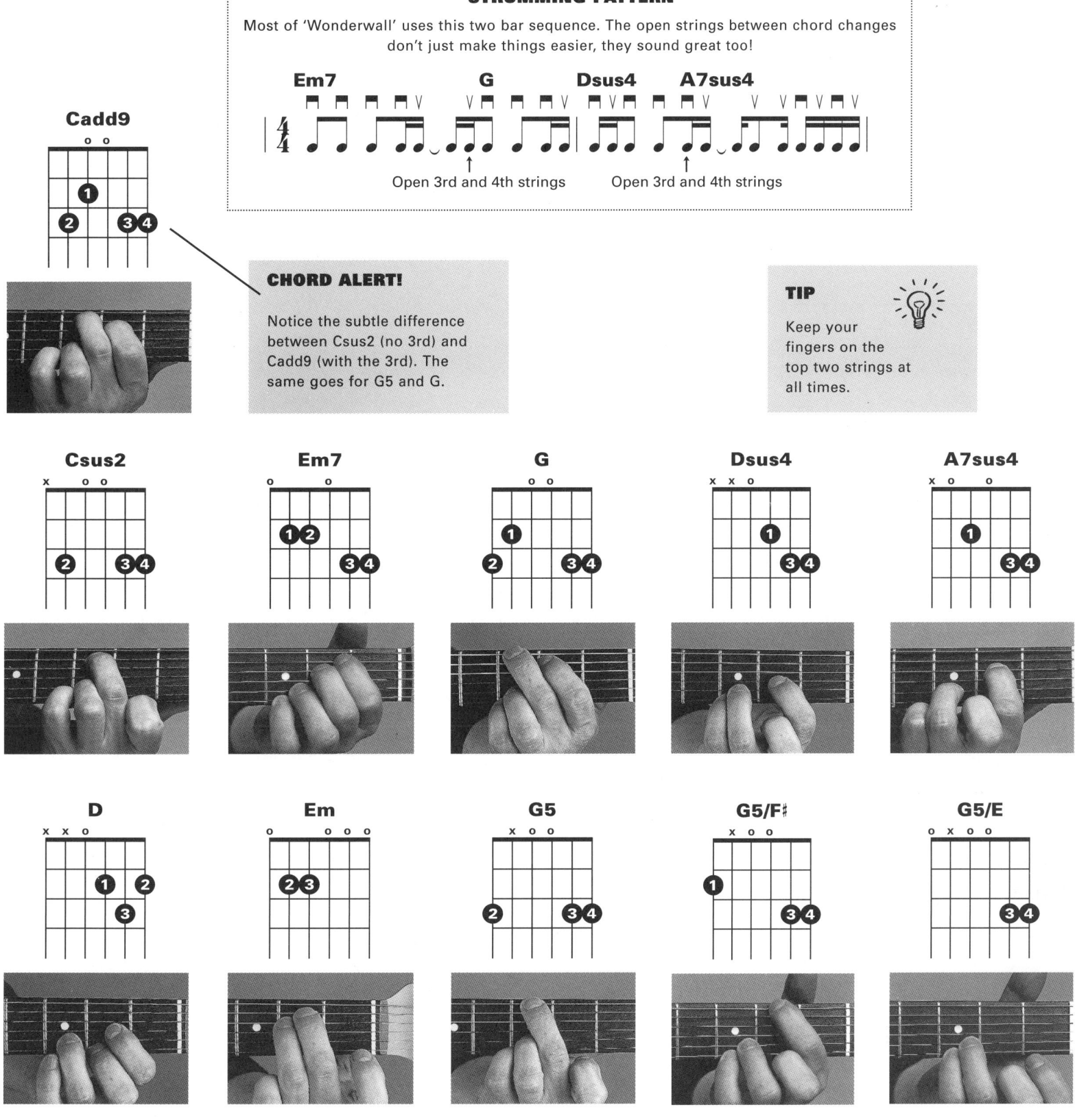

CHORD ALERT! Notice the subtle difference between Csus2 (no 3rd) and Cadd9 (with the 3rd). The same goes for G5 and G.

TIP Keep your fingers on the top two strings at all times.

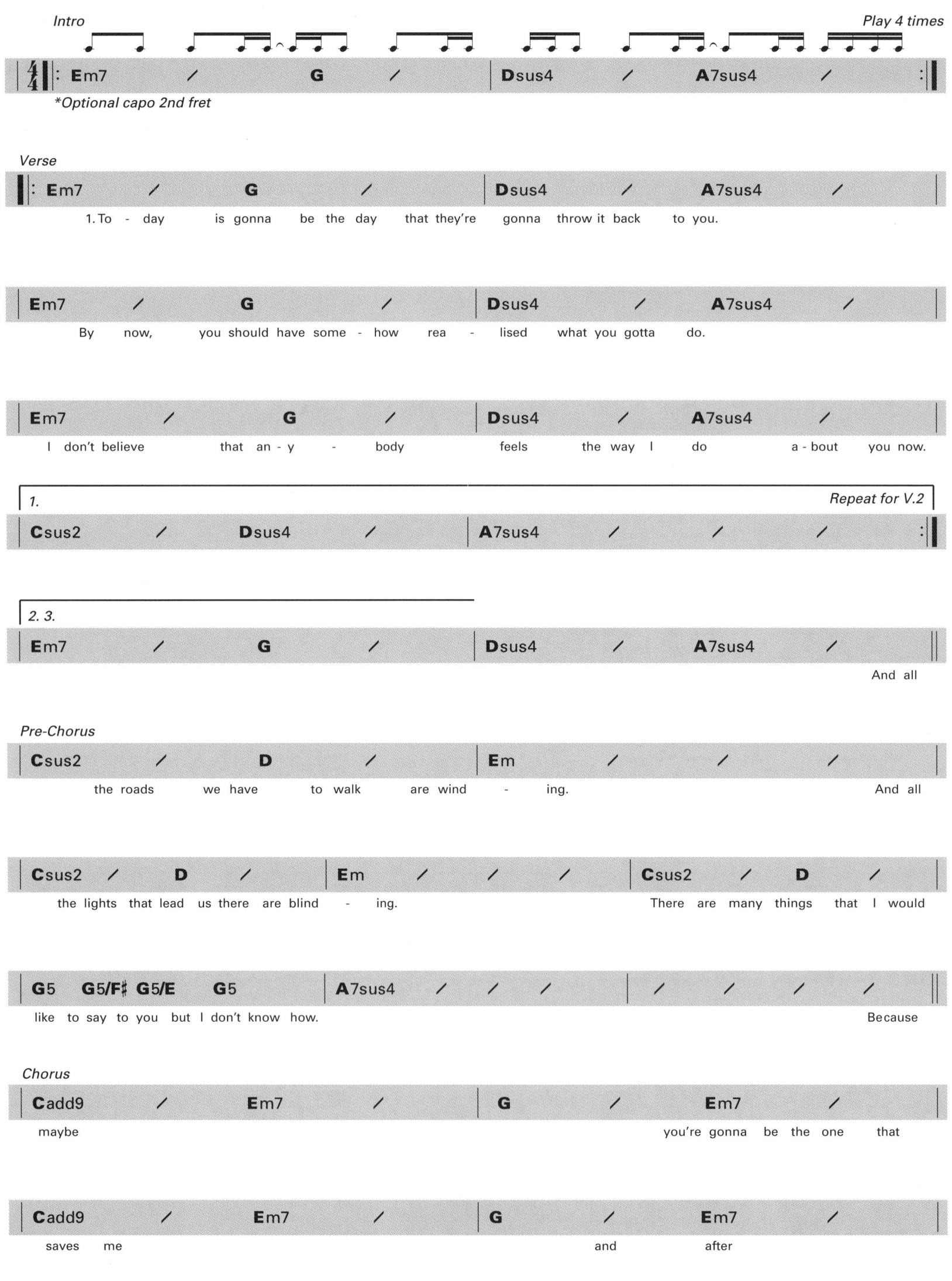

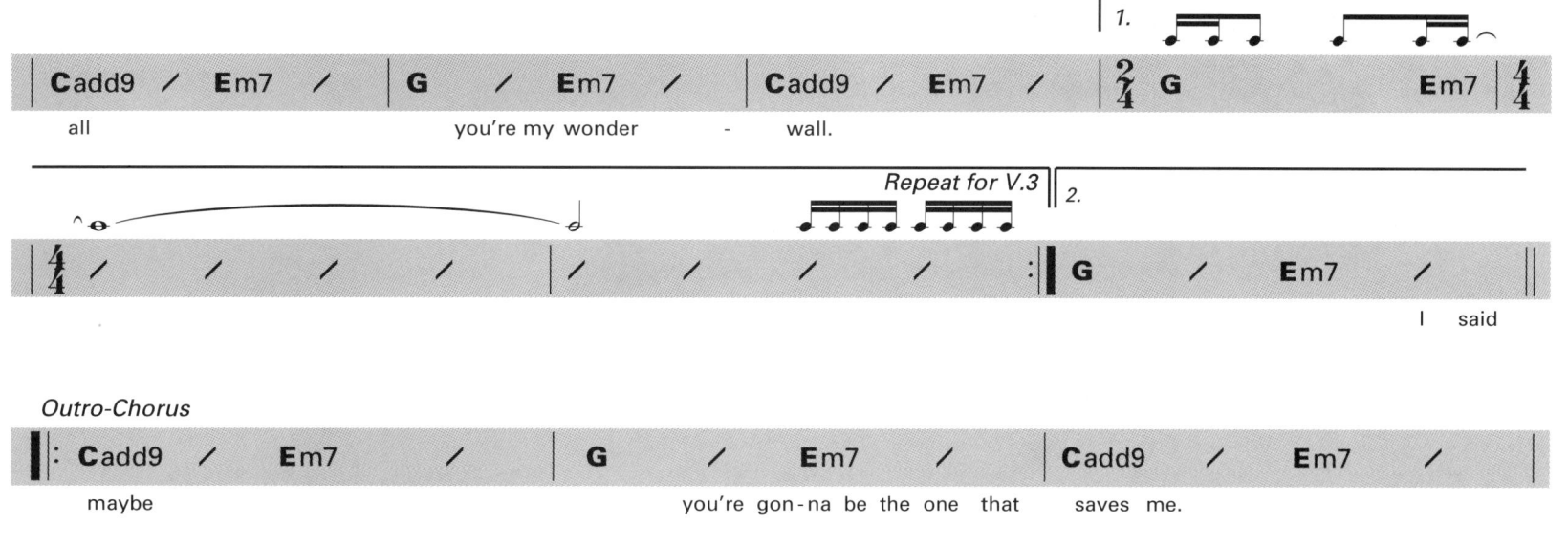

Outro-Chorus

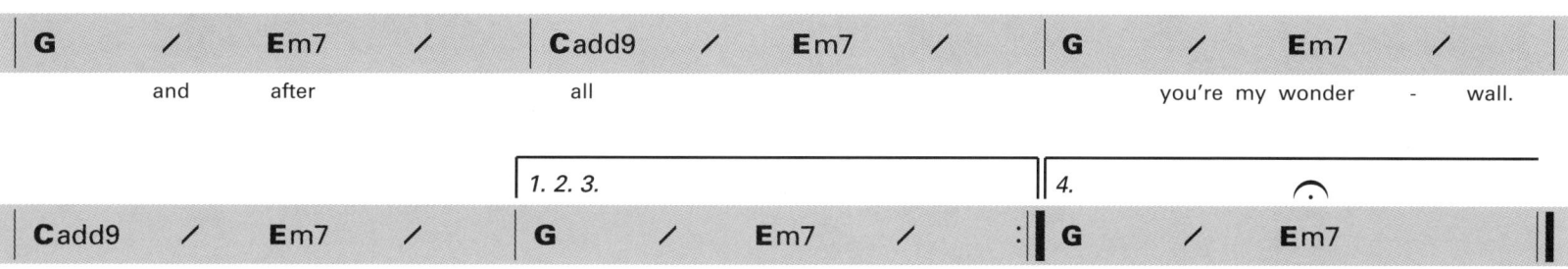

| G | / | Em7 | / | Cadd9 | / | Em7 | / | G | / | Em7 | / |

and after all you're my wonder - wall.

| Cadd9 | / | Em7 | / | G | / | Em7 | / : | G | / | Em7 | |

I said

VERSE 2

Back beat, the word is on the street
That the fire in your heart is out
I'm sure you've heard it all before
But you never really had a doubt
I don't believe that anybody feels the way I do
About you now.

VERSE 3

Today was gonna be the day
But they're gonna throw it back to you
By now, you should have somehow
Realised what you gotta do
I don't believe that anybody feels the way I do
About you now.

PRE-CHORUS 2

And all the roads that lead you there were winding
And all the lights that light the way are blinding
There are many things that I would like to say to you
But I don't know how.

Words & Music by Noel Gallagher

© Copyright 1995 Oasis Music, Creation Songs Limited & Sony/ATV Music Publishing
(UK) Limited, 10 Great Marlborough Street, London W1.
All Rights Reserved. International Copyright Secured.

The Fool On The Hill

Exploring The Added 6th

CHORD CHECK
See *Chord Chemistry* pages 16 & 17.

This Paul McCartney track from the Beatles' *Magical Mystery Tour* extravaganza features primarily a piano accompaniment which can be easily adapted to play on an acoustic guitar.

Compare these different voicings of **D6**: and some possibilities for **Em7/D**:

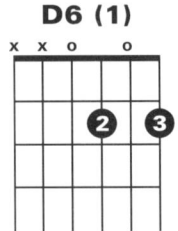 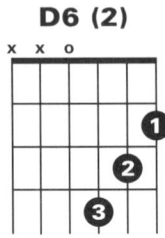 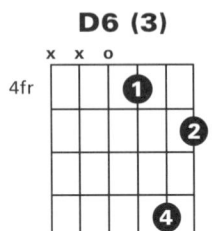 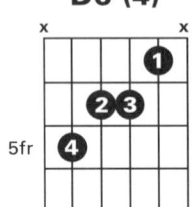 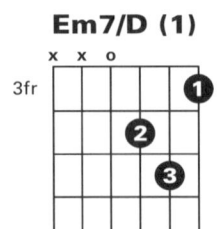 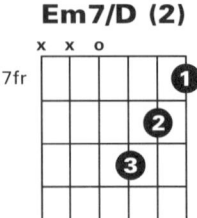

You'll notice that some progressions work better (and are easier to play) than others. The choice depends on the chord progression – notice the choice of **D6** and **Em7/D** in various parts of the song – but experiment with the others.

TIP
The /D refers to the bass note of the chord – hence the open D string.

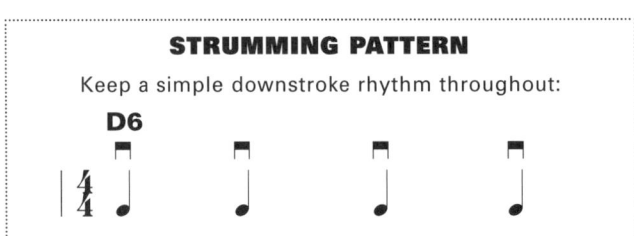

STRUMMING PATTERN
Keep a simple downstroke rhythm throughout:

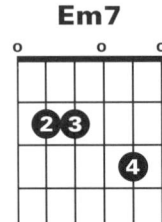
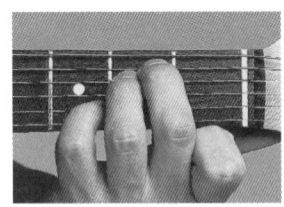

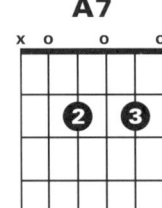
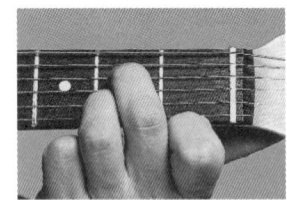

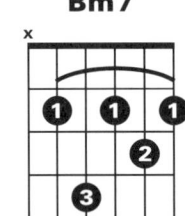
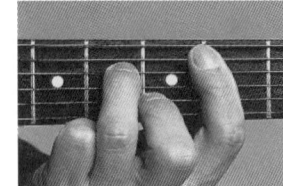

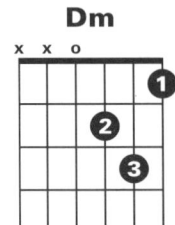

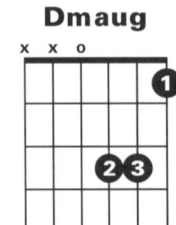
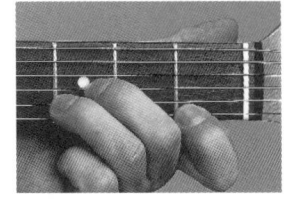

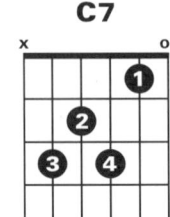
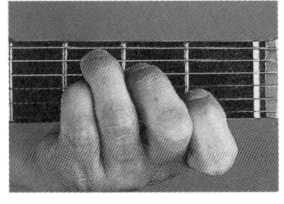

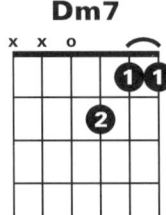
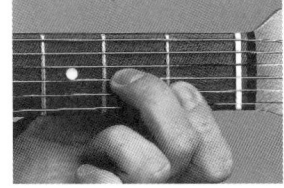

20 CHORD CHEMISTRY SONGBOOK

Intro

| **D**6 (3) / / / | / / / / |

Verse

‖: **D**6 (2) / / / | / / / / | **E**m7/**D** (2) / / / | / / / / |

1. Day af - ter day   a - lone   on a hill,   the

| **D**6 (3) / / / | / / / / | **E**m7/**D** (2) / / / | / / / / |

man with the fool - ish grin is keep - ing perfect - ly still.   But

| **E**m7 / / / | **A**7 / / / | **D**6 (4) / / / | **B**m7 / / / |

no - bo - dy wants to know him,   they can see that he's just a fool,   and

Chorus

| **E**m7 / / / | **A**7 / / / | **D**m / **D**m aug / | **D**m / / / |

he ne - ver gives an an - swer. But the   fool on the hill   sees the sun

| **D**m aug / / / | / / / / | **C**7 / / / | / / / / |

     go - ing down   and the eyes   in his head   see the world

Repeat for Verses 2, 3 & 4

| **D**m / / / | **D**m7 / / / | **D**6 (1) / / / | / / / / :‖

     spin - ning 'round.

Outro   *Repeat to fade*

‖: **D**6 (1) / / / | / / / / | **E**m7/**D** (1) / / / | / / / / :‖

Oh,   'round,   'round,   'round,   'round.

VERSE 2

Well on the way, alone on a hill
The man with the foolish grin
Is keeping perfectly still
But nobody even hears him or the
Sound he appears to make
And he never seems to notice.
But the fool on the hill...

VERSE 3

Oh, oh, oh, oh, oh
'round, 'round
'round, 'round, 'round
And nobody seems to like him
They can tell what he wants to do
And he never shows his feelings.
But the fool on the hill...

VERSE 4

Oh, oh, oh, oh, oh
'round, 'round
'round, 'round, 'round
And he never listens to them
He knows that they're the fools
But they don't like him.
The fool on the hill...

Words & Music by John Lennon & Paul McCartney
© Copyright 1967 Northern Songs.
All Rights Reserved. International Copyright Secured.

Papa's Got A Brand New Bag (Pt. 1)

CHORD CHECK

See *Chord Chemistry* page 22.

The Famous 9th shape

This was Jimmy Nolen's début session with James Brown. The track was recorded in under an hour by an exhausted band who had stopped at the studio en-route between gigs. The track (originally called 'Papa's Got A Brand New Drag') was too slow and had to be sped up, changing the key from E♭ to E! One of the most recognisable guitar parts in popular music occurs in the 11th and 12th bars – Nolen's jangly **E9** chord voicing which became synonymous with many James Brown classics.

E9 TOP TIP

Concentrate on playing the top three strings to get that tight jangly sound!

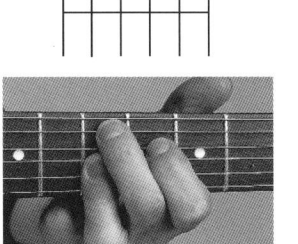

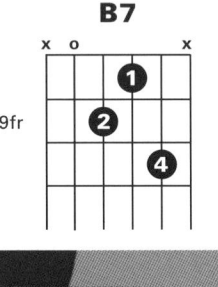

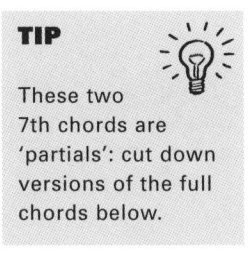

TIP

These two 7th chords are 'partials': cut down versions of the full chords below.

These are the full **A7** and **B7** chord versions:

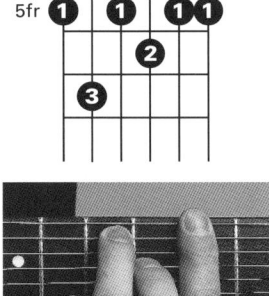

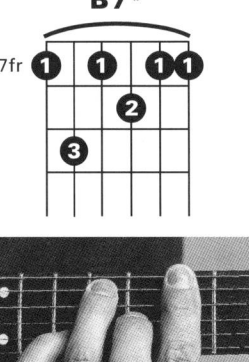

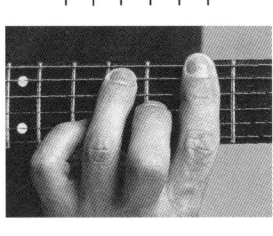

The rhythm throughout the main part of the song is simple, just downstrokes on beat 2 and 4 in each bar. A proper R&B backbeat requires that the chord is instantly deadened by releasing the left hand finger pressure – don't let it ring on! (A good rhythm should disappear into the back of the track with the attack of the snare drum.)

The rhythm in bars 11 & 12 and 32 & 33 should be played with up and down strokes:

NOTE:

Play the full B7 chord (B7*) after each E9 sequence.

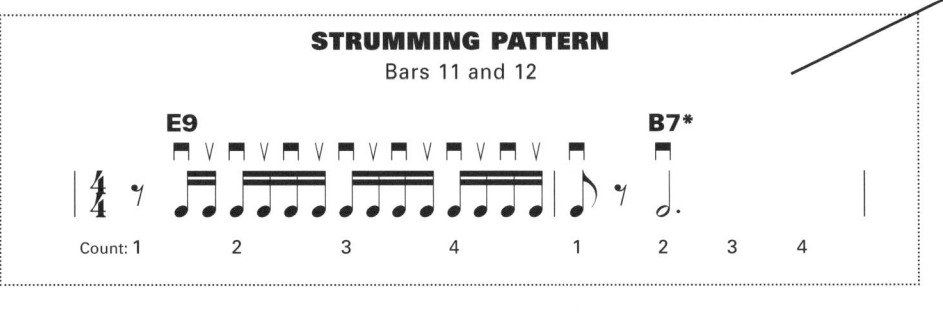

22   **CHORD CHEMISTRY SONGBOOK**

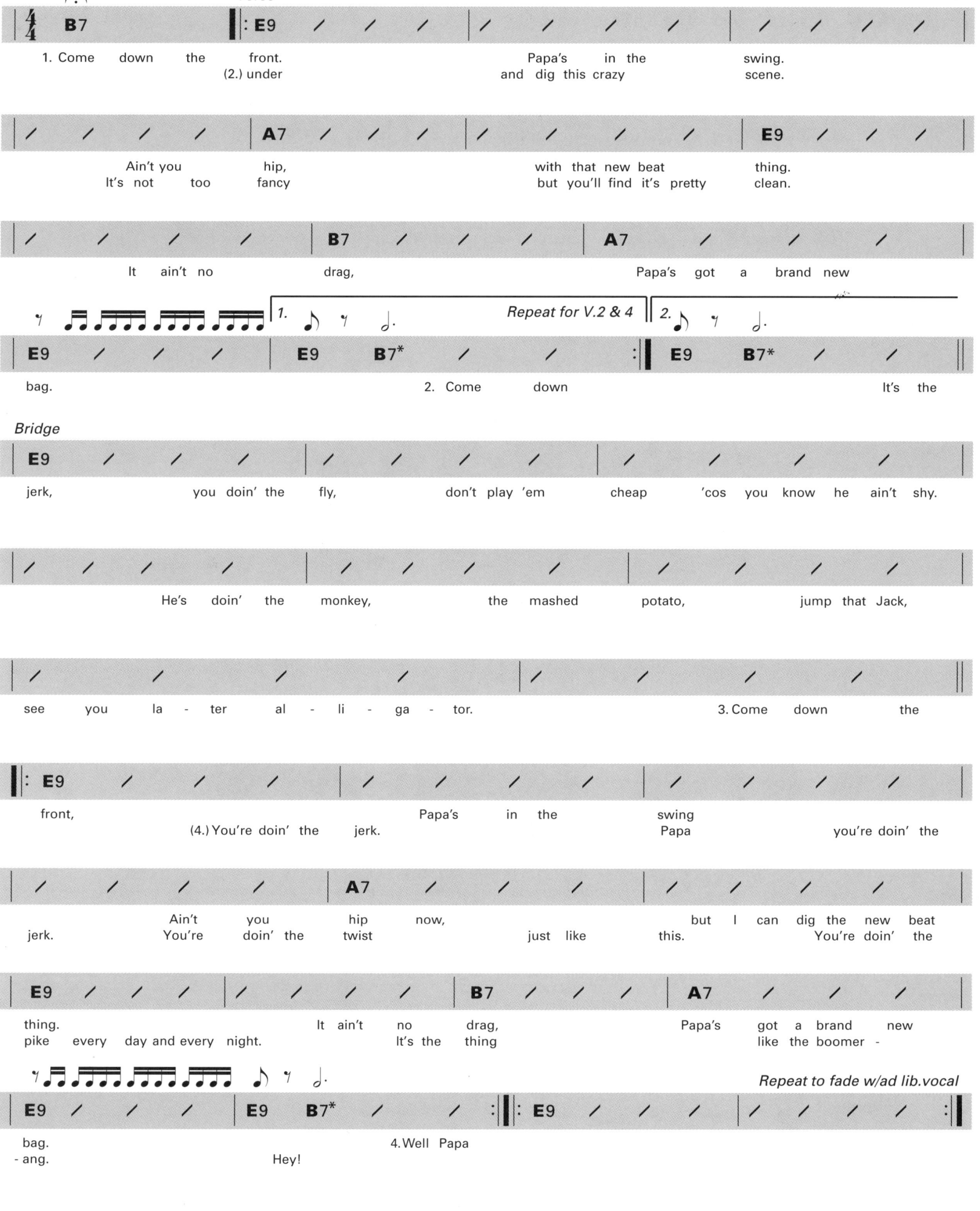

Words & Music by James Brown
© Copyright 1965 Dynatone Publishing Company & Jadar Music Corporation, USA.
Warner Chappell Music Limited, Griffin House, 161 Hammersmith Road, London W6.
All Rights Reserved. International Copyright Secured.

I Shot The Sheriff

Exploring Minor Chords

CHORD CHECK

See *Chord Chemistry* page 24,25 & 47.

Bob Marley's reggae standard was originally recorded for the Wailers' *Burnin'* album, and later by Eric Clapton who took it to the top of the US charts. This is a great workout for practising those minor chord shapes as well as your rhythm chops!

To keep the rhythm tight, concentrate on playing only the upper part of the chord, ie: a partial chord (see James Brown's 'Papa's Got A Brand New Bag' on page 22).

VERSE CHORDS

Play the top three strings of each chord.

CHORUS CHORDS

Again, concentrate on the top three strings.

TIP

Here's a simpler alternative to the barred Dm chord.

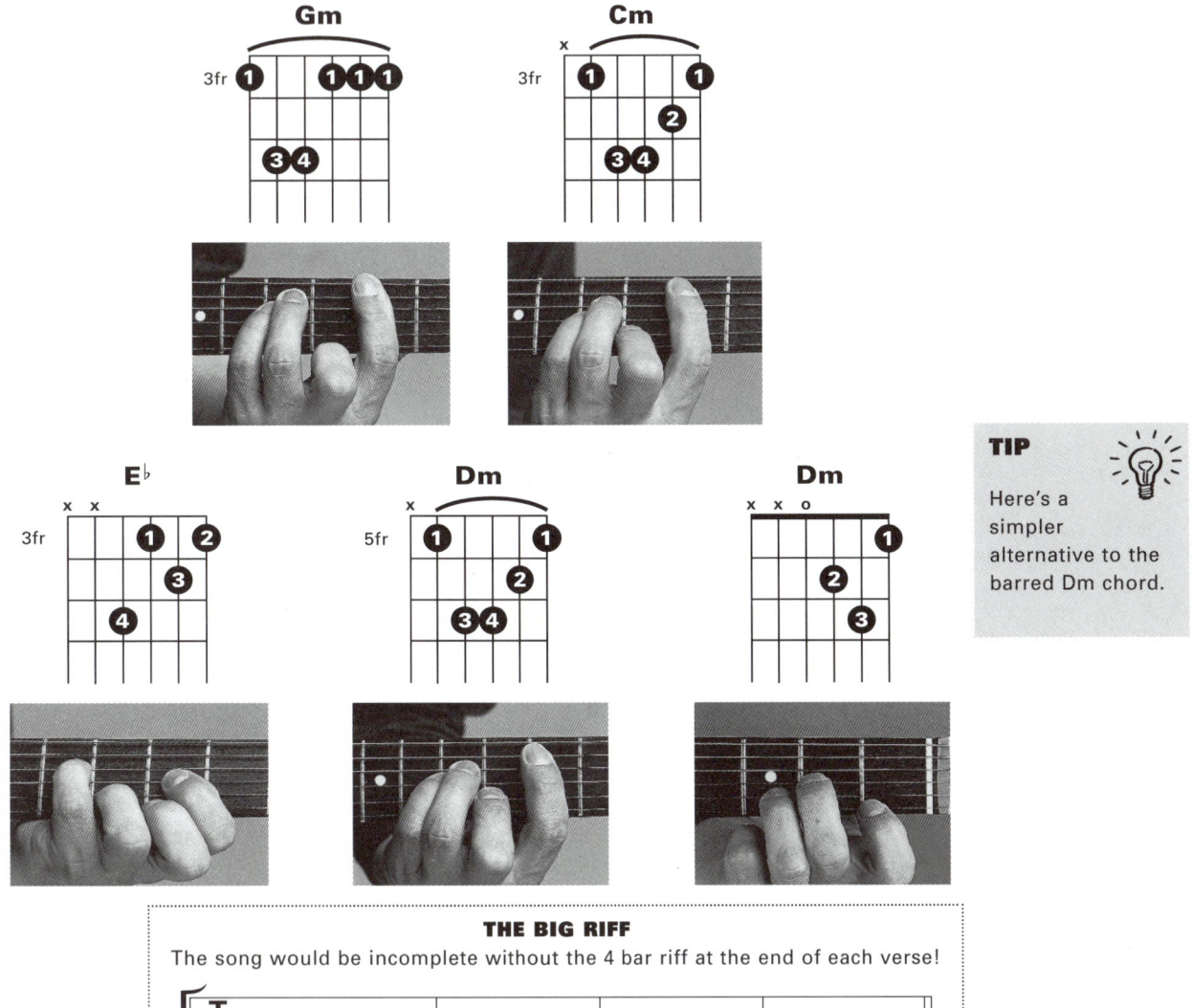

THE BIG RIFF
The song would be incomplete without the 4 bar riff at the end of each verse!

STRUMMING PATTERN
Rhythm Alert! Count the chorus and verse rhythms as follows and play with a swing feel:

Chorus

| **Gm** / / / | / / / / | **Cm** / / / | / / / / |

I shot the sher - iff,   but I did - n't shoot the

| **Gm** / / / | / / / / | / / / / | / / / / :|

de - pu - ty,   oh,   no,   oh.

% *Verse*

| **E♭** / / / | **Dm** / / / | **Gm** / / / | / / / / |

1. All a - round in my home town   they're

| **E♭** / / / | **Dm** / / / | **Gm** / / / | / / / / |

tryin' to track me down,   yeah.   They

| **E♭** / / / | **Dm** / / / | **Gm** / / / | / / / / |

say they want to bring me in guil - ty,   for the

| **E♭** / / / | **Dm** / / / | **Gm** / / / | / / / / |

killing of a dep - u - ty,   for the

Play 3 times
Repeat for Ch. 2, V. 2, Ch. 3, V. 3

| **E♭** / / / | **Dm** / / / | **Gm** / / / | / / / / |

life of a dep - u - ty.   But I say,

Riff

| **Gm** / / / | / / / / | / / / / | / / / / |

D.%. for V.4 then rpt. chorus ad lib. to fade

| / / / / | / / / / :| — 4 — ‖

oh now now.

CHORUS 2

I shot the sheriff
But I swear it was in self-defence
I said, I shot the sheriff
Lord, and they said it was a capital offence
Hear this...

VERSE 2

Sheriff John Brown always hated me
For what I don't know
Ev'ry time I plant a seed
He said, kill it before it grows
He said, kill it before they grow, and so...

VERSE 3

Freedom came my way one day
And I started out of town, yeah
All of a sudden I saw Sheriff John Brown
Aimin' to shoot me down
So I shot, I shot him down, and I say...

VERSE 4 (%)

Reflexes had the better of me
And what it is to be must be
Ev'ry day the bucket ago a well
One day the bottom ago drop out
One day the bottom ago drop out.

Words & Music by Bob Marley
© Copyright 1974 Cayman Music Incorporated, USA.
Blue Mountain Music Limited, 8 Kensington Park Road, London W11.
All Rights Reserved. International Copyright Secured.

How Deep Is Your Love

More Minor Chords

> **CHORD CHECK**
>
> See *Chord Chemistry* page 26.

Time to show off your falsetto voice as well as your chord playing with this Bee Gees ballad from *Saturday Night Fever*, the best selling film soundtrack ever.

To play this track in its original key (E♭), use a capo at the 3rd fret.

C **Em7** 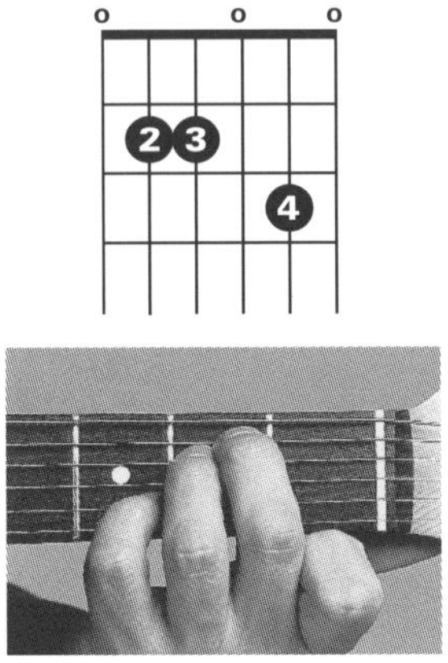 **Dm7** 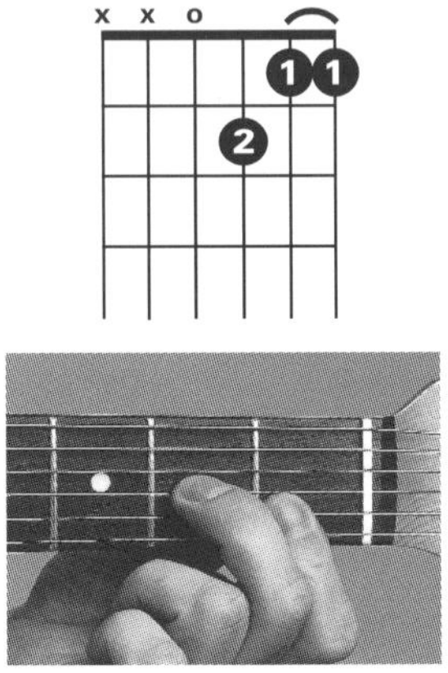 **A7** 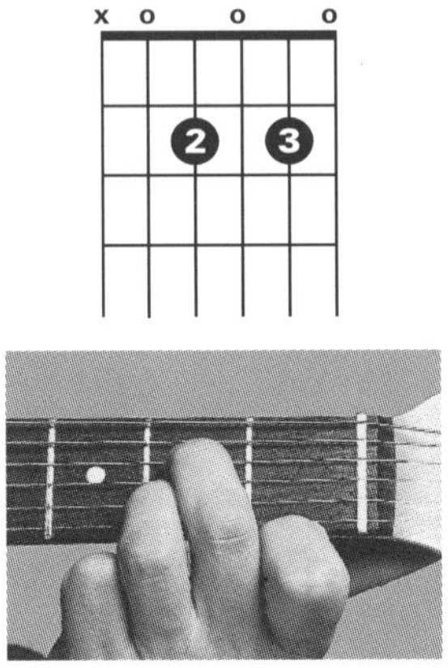 **E7**

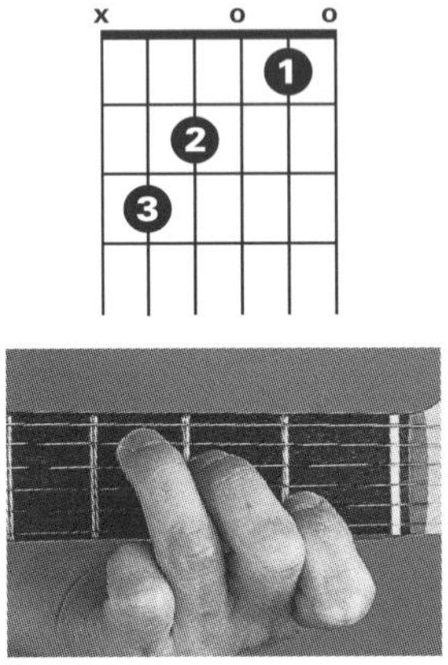

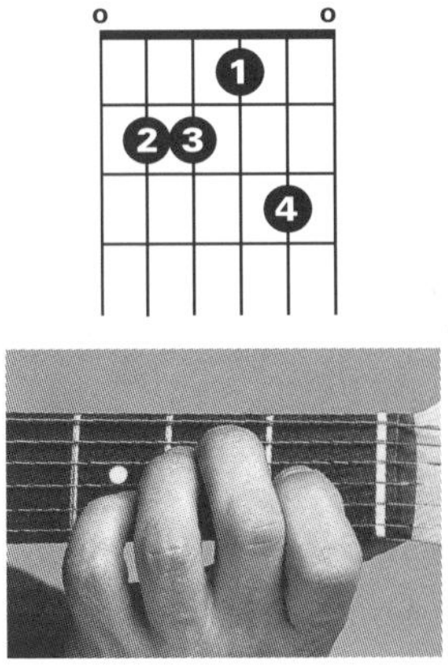

> 💡 **TIP**
>
> The slash /G refers to the bass note. This chord is F with a G in the bass.

F/G **G7** 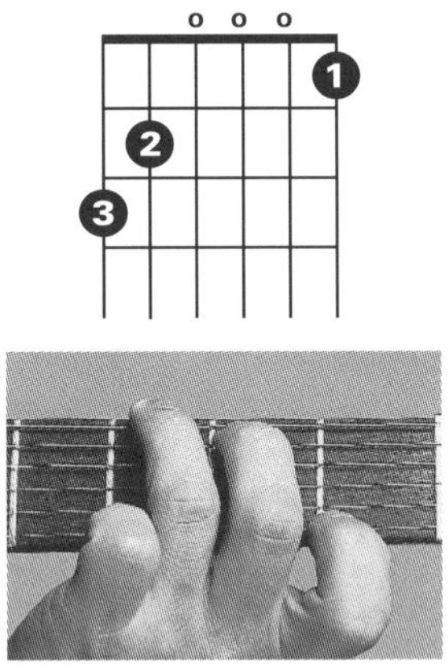 **Am7** 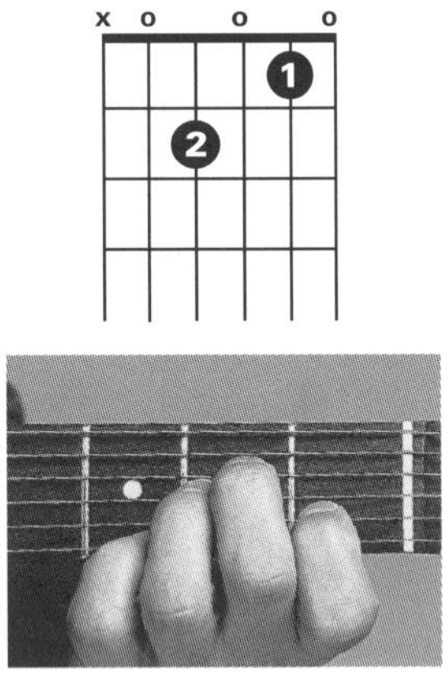 **Fmaj7** 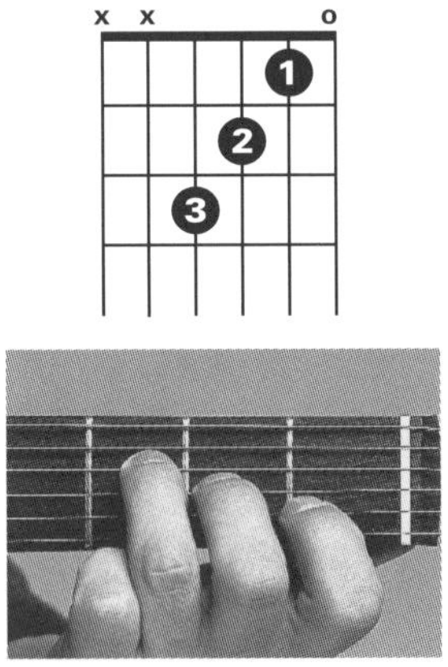 **B♭9**

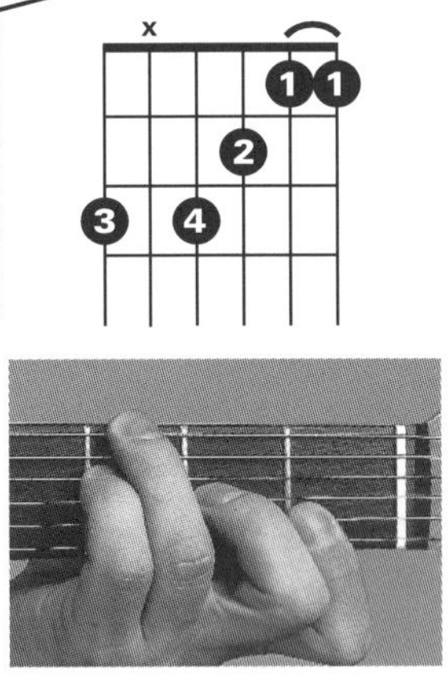

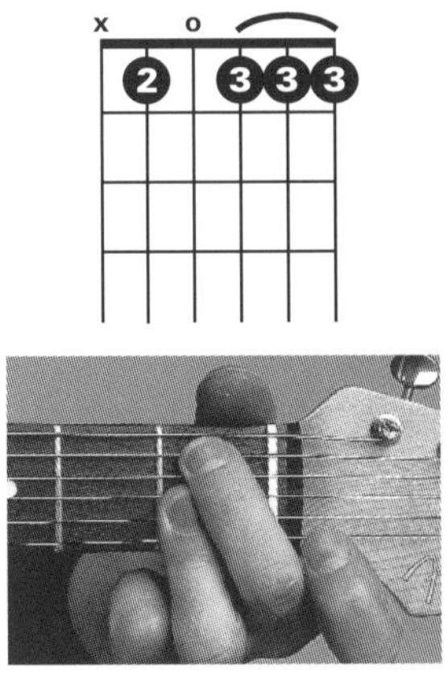

Cmaj7 **Fm6** **Gm/B♭**

> **MINOR 6**
>
> The Minor 6th is a beautiful sounding chord, check out this voicing too:
>
> (See *Chord Chemistry* pages 30 & 31.)
>
> **Fm6**

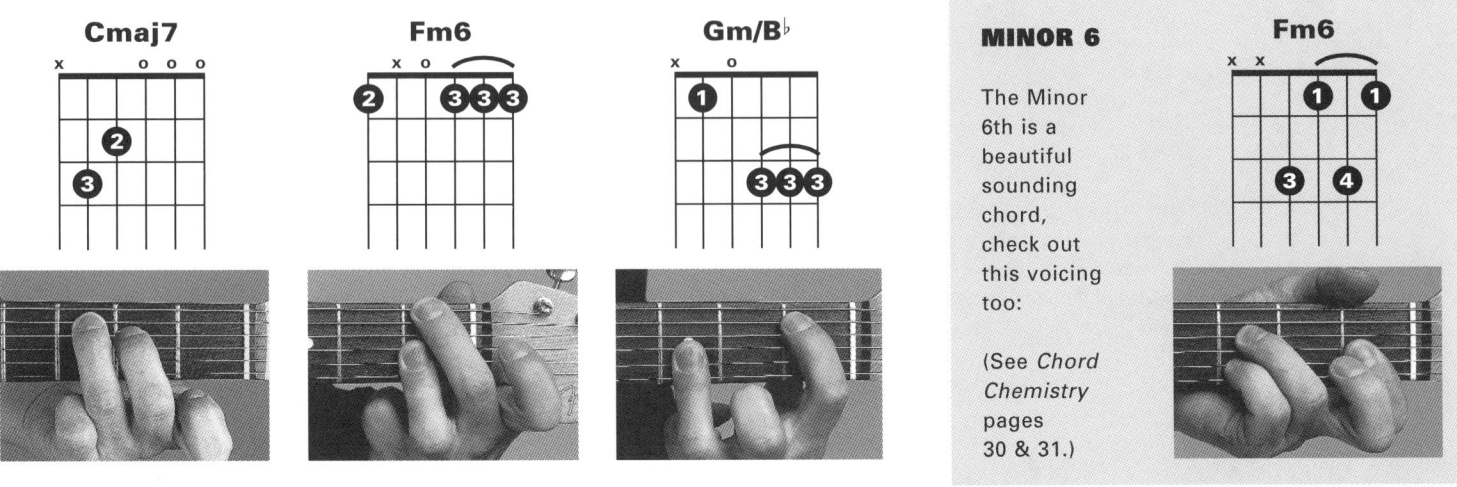

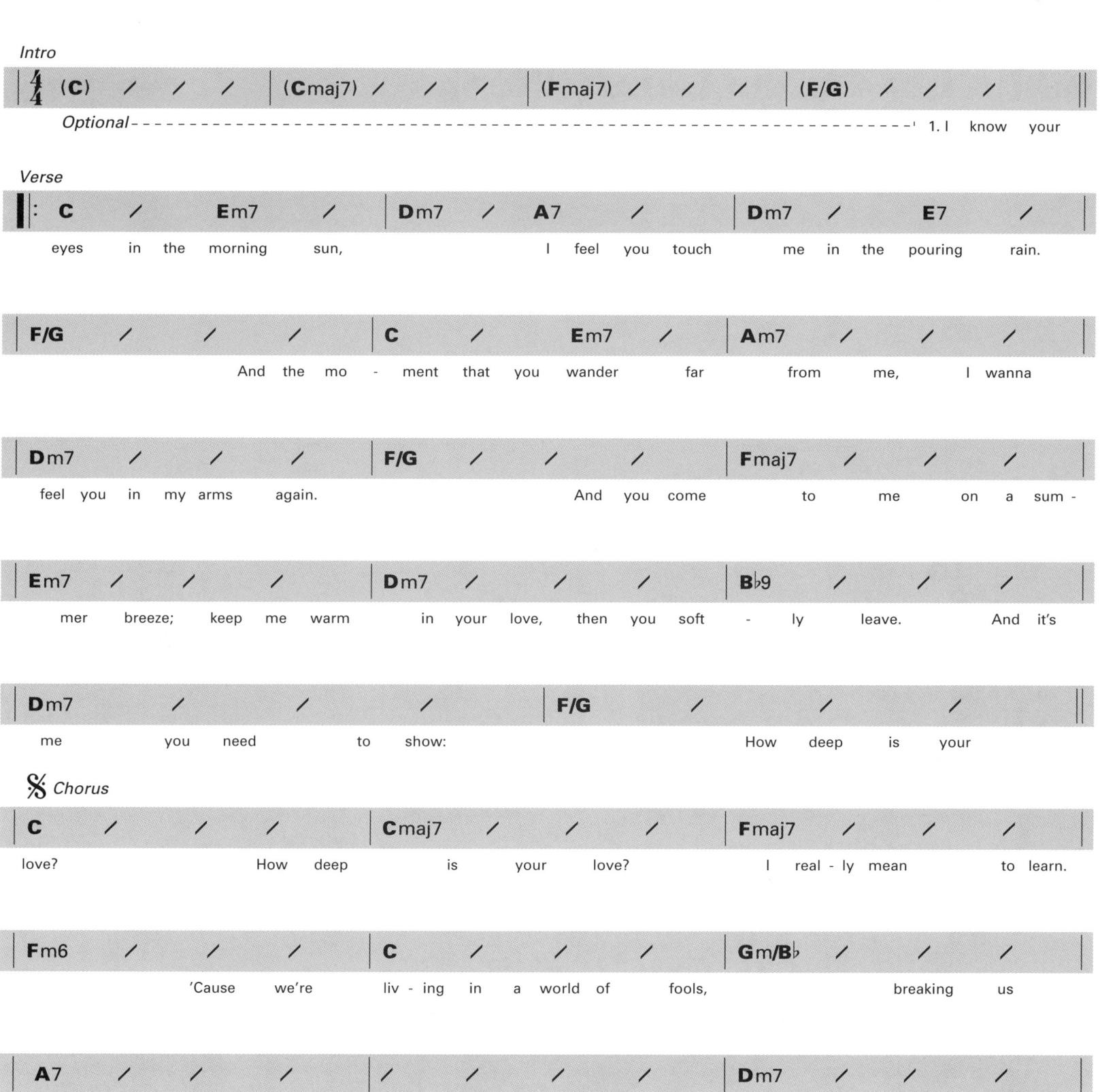

VERSE 2

I believe in you
You know the door to my very soul
You're the light in my deepest, darkest hour
You're my saviour when I fall.
And you may not think that I care for you
When you know down inside that I really do
And it's me you need to show...

Words & Music by Barry Gibb, Robin Gibb & Maurice Gibb
© Copyright 1977 Gibb Brothers Music.
All Rights Reserved. International Copyright Secured.

While My Guitar Gently Weeps

The Descending Minor Progression

CHORD CHECK

See *Chord Chemistry*
pages 30-31

This George Harrison track from The Beatles' *White Album* was first recorded with a simple acoustic guitar accompaniment. Although the chords don't strictly follow the descending **Am** progression, the **D9/F♯** is very similar to **Am/F♯** – check out the difference. You may also notice that **Fmaj7** could also be called **Am/F** – they've got the same notes, but in a different order.

NOTE

The open A string is muted in each of the slash chords.

TIP

D9/F♯ is easier to finger than Am/F♯, but take care not to mute the open D string.

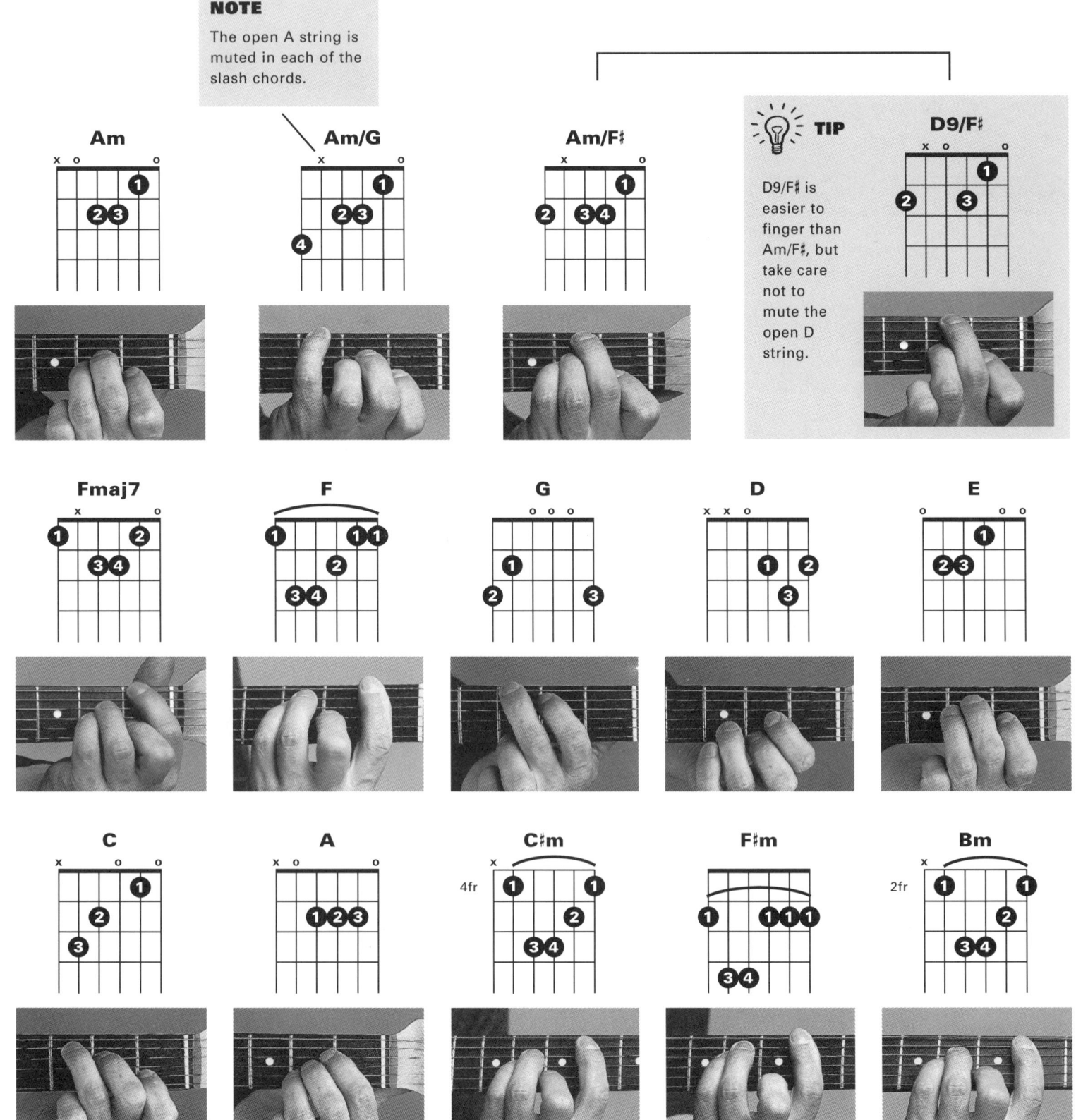

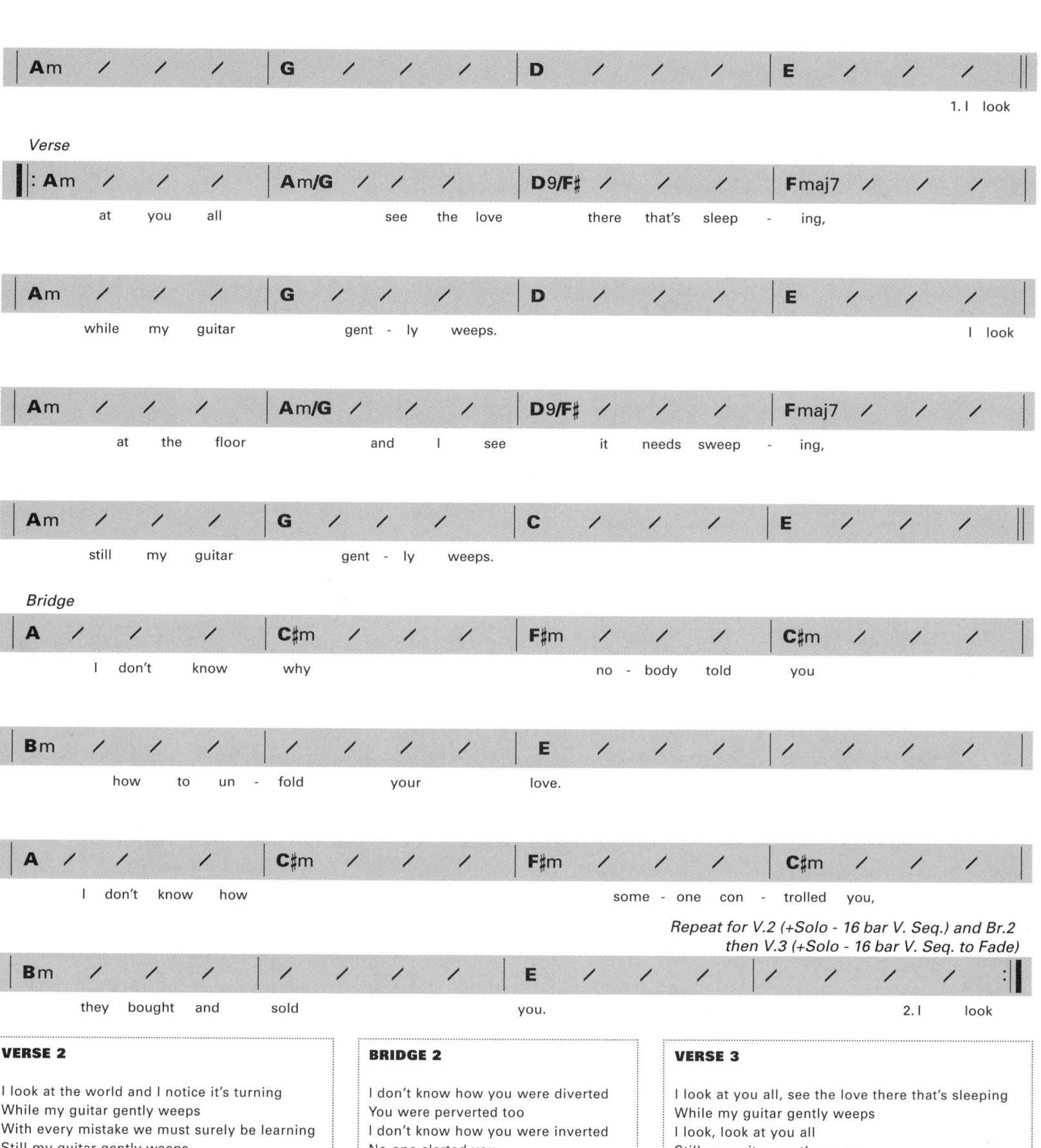

VERSE 2

I look at the world and I notice it's turning
While my guitar gently weeps
With every mistake we must surely be learning
Still my guitar gently weeps.

BRIDGE 2

I don't know how you were diverted
You were perverted too
I don't know how you were inverted
No one alerted you.

VERSE 3

I look at you all, see the love there that's sleeping
While my guitar gently weeps
I look, look at you all
Still my guitar gently weeps.

Words & Music by George Harrison
© Copyright 1968 Harrisongs Limited.
All Rights Reserved. International Copyright Secured.

Tears In Heaven

Exploring Slash Chords

> **CHORD CHECK**
>
> See *Chord Chemistry* pages 35-37

Eric Clapton's beautiful ballad featured on the hugely successful *MTV Unplugged* recording and is a model piece for demonstrating a chord progression using slash chords. Originally played fingerstyle on a nylon classical guitar, the song requires the most delicate touch. We've shown photographs of the slash chords you'll need in order to play this song, and diagrams of the rest of the chords are shown below.

> **TIP**
>
> A/E and E7* are 'partial' chords: check out *Chord Chemistry* page 50.

> **TIP**
>
> The fingering of this A chord makes it easier to add the decorative Sus4 and to move to E/G#.

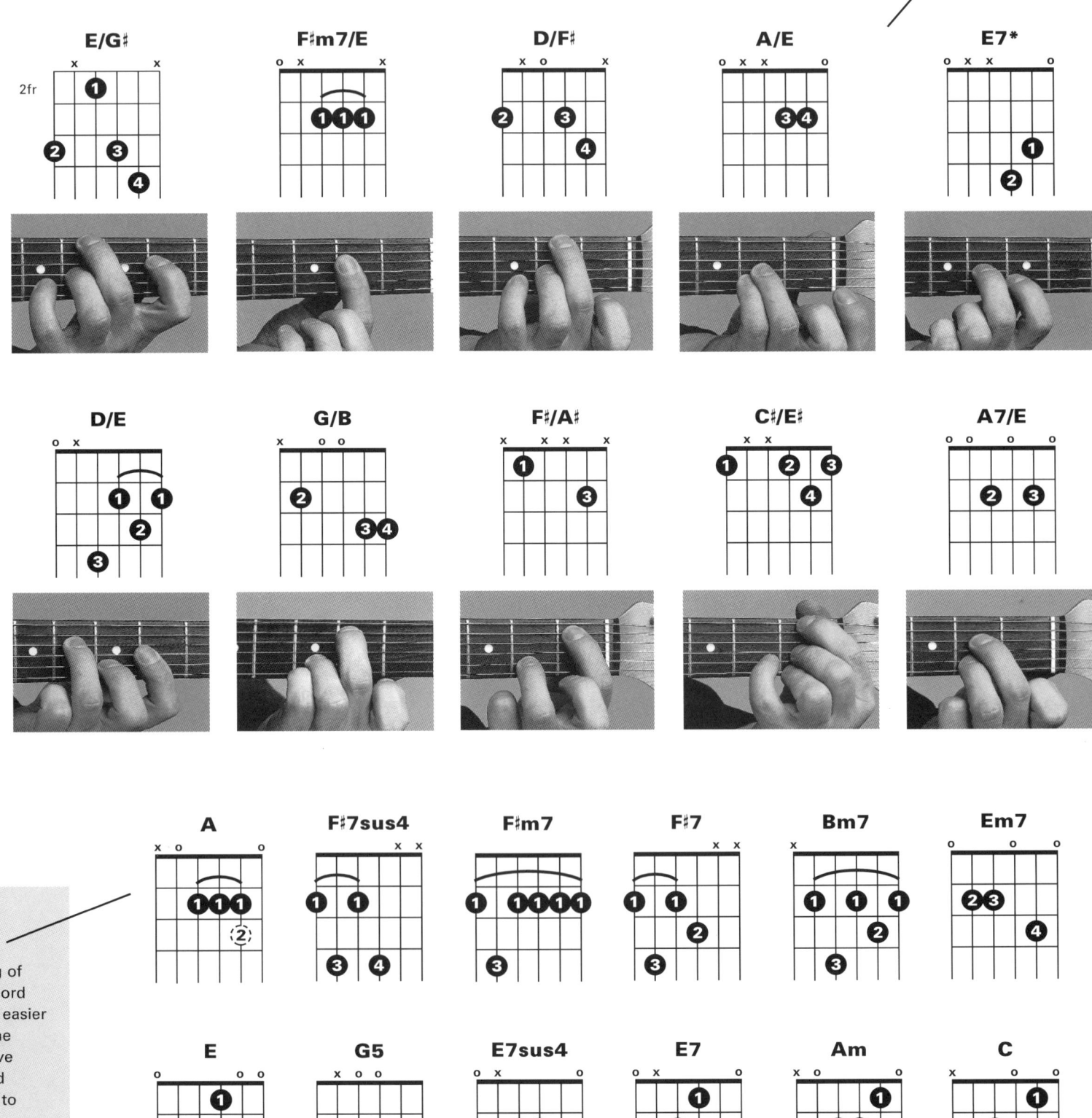

30 CHORD CHEMISTRY SONGBOOK

Intro

| 4/4 A | / | E/G# | / | F#m7 | / | F#m7/E | / | D/F# | / | E7sus4 | E7 | A | / | / | / |

%% Verse

| A | / | E/G# | / | F#m7 | / | F#m7/E | / | D/F# | / | A | / |

Would you know   my name   if I saw you in hea-

| E | / | A/E | E7* | A | / | E/G# | / | F#m7 | / | F#m7/E | / |

-ven?   Would it be   the same

| D/F# | / | A/E | / | E | / | A/E | E7* |

if I saw you in hea - ven?

| F#m7 | / | / | / | C#/E# | / | / | / | A7/E | / | / | / |

I must be strong   and car - ry on,

To Coda ⊕

| F#7 | / | F#7sus4 | F#/A# | Bm7 | / | / | / | D/E | / | / | / |

'cause I know   I don't belong   here in hea-

| A | / | E/G# | / | F#m7 | / | F#m7/E | / | D/F# | / | E7sus4 | E7 |

-ven.

Bridge

| A | / | / | / | : | C | / | G/B | / | Am | / | D/F# | / |

Time can bring   you down,   time can bend   your knees.

| G5 | / | D/F# | / | Em7 | / | D/F# | G5 | C | / | G/B | / |

Time can break   your heart,

D.%. al Coda
w/repeats (1° Gtr. Solo, 2° V.3)

| Am | / | D/F# | / | G5 | / | D/F# | / | E | / | A/E | E7* |

have you beggin'   please.

⊕ Coda

| A | / | E/G# | / | F#m7 | / | F#m7/E | / | D/F# | / | E7sus4 | E7 | A |

-ven   *rit. (slow down)- - - - - - - - - - -*

VERSE 2

Would you hold my hand
If I saw you in heaven?
Would you help me stand
If I saw you in heaven?

I'll find my way
Through night and day
'Cause I know I just can't stay
Here in heaven.

VERSE 3 (%)

Would you know my name
If I saw you in heaven?
Would you do the same
If I saw you in heaven?

I must be strong
And carry on
'Cause I know I don't belong
Here in heaven.

Words & Music by Eric Clapton & Will Jennings. © Copyright 1991 & 1995 E.C. Music Limited, London NW1 (87.5%).
© Copyright 1991 Blue Sky Rider Songs administered by Rondor Music (London) Limited, 10a Parsons Green, London SW6 for the World
(excluding the USA & Canada) (12.5%). All Rights Reserved. International Copyright Secured.

Michelle

> **CHORD CHECK**
>
> See *Chord Chemistry* page 47.

Moveable Minor Shapes

Paul McCartney's classic ballad from the Beatles' *Rubber Soul* album features two acoustic guitars capoed at the 5th fret. The boxes below show the chords in their non-capoed positions with corresponding chord names – by using a capo at the 5th fret, the song moves up a fourth – for example **Cm** becomes **Fm**, and **A♭maj7** becomes **D♭maj7** and so on.

> 💡 **KNOWLEDGEABLE FACT**
>
> Paul McCartney only played the top three strings in the 'Cminor' chord progression.

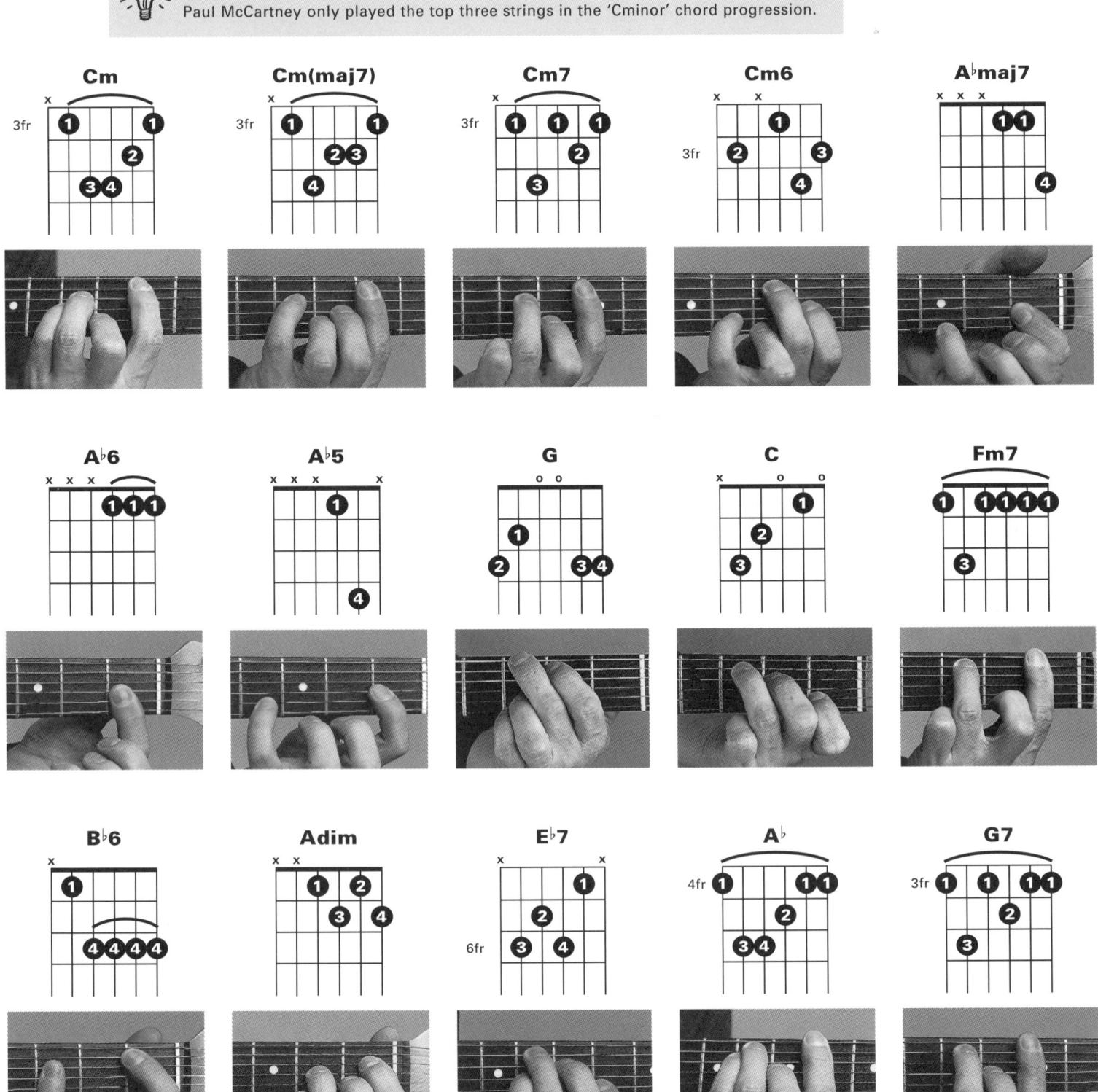

Intro

Capo 5th fret

| **C**m | **C**m(maj7) | **C**m7 | **C**m6 | **A**♭maj7 | **A**♭6 **A**♭5 | **G** |

Chorus

| **C** | **F**m7 | **B**♭6 | **A**dim |

1. Mi - chelle, ma belle, these are words that go to - geth - er

| **G** **A**dim | **G** | **C** | **F**m7 |

well, my Michelle. Mi - chelle, ma belle,

| **B**♭6 | **A**dim | **G** **A**dim | **G** |

sont les mots qui vont trés bien en - semble, trés bien en - semble. 1. I

Verse

| **C**m | | **E**♭7 | **A**♭ |

love you, I love you, I love you, that's all I want to say.

| **G**7 | **C**m | **C**m **C**m(maj7) |

Un - til I find a way, I will say the on - ly

| **C**m7 **C**m6 | **A**♭maj7 **A**♭6 **A**♭5 | **G** |

words I know that you'll un - der - stand.

Chorus

| **C** | **F**m7 | **B**♭6 | **A**dim |

2. Mi - chelle, ma belle, sont les mots qui vont trés bien en -

1. 2. — *Rpt. for V.2+3* — *3.*

| **G** **A**dim | **G** | | **G** |

- semble, trés bien en - semble. 2. I - semble. And I will

D.%.
with Gtr. solo and fade through Chorus

| **C**m **C**m(maj7) | **C**m7 **C**m6 | **A**♭maj7 **A**♭6 **A**♭5 | **G** |

say the on - ly words I know that you'll un - der - stand, my Michelle.

VERSE 2

I need to, I need to, I need to
I need to make you see
Oh, what you mean to me
Until I do I'm hoping you will
Know what I mean.

VERSE 3

I want you, I want you, I want you
I think you know by now
I'll get to you somehow
Until I do, I'm telling you
So you'll understand.

CHORUS 3

(Guitar Solo)

CHORUS 4

(As Chorus 2)

Words & Music by John Lennon & Paul McCartney
© Copyright 1965 Northern Songs.
All Rights Reserved. International Copyright Secured.

Hush

> **CHORD CHECK**
>
> See *Chord Chemistry*
> page 55.

The 7♯9 Chord

You better get your rhythm chops together for this one – Kula Shaker's burning version of Deep Purple's classic rocker. The song demonstrates the **7♯9** chord in two positions, but first, check out the underlying rhythm in the song.

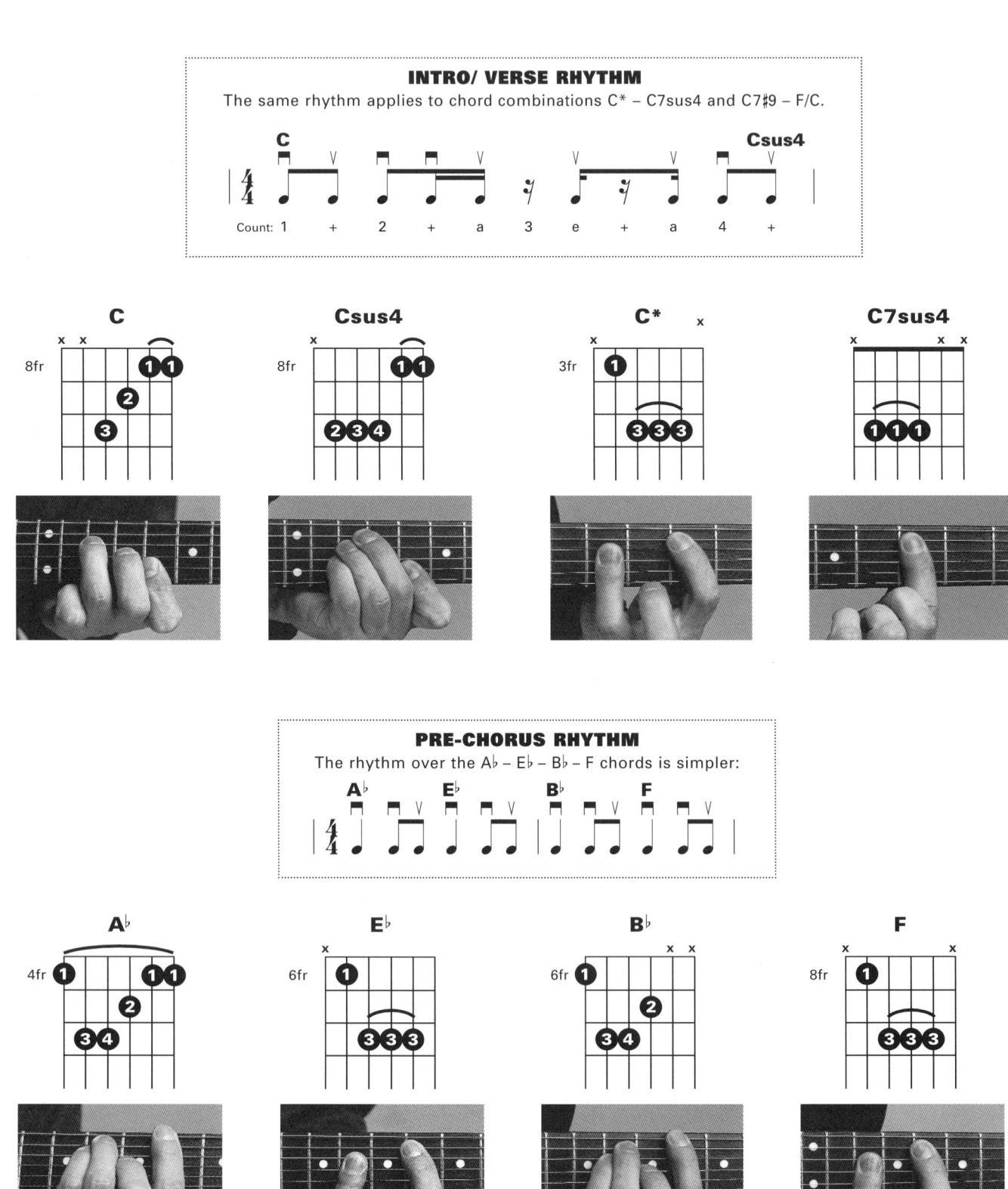

CHORD CHEMISTRY SONGBOOK

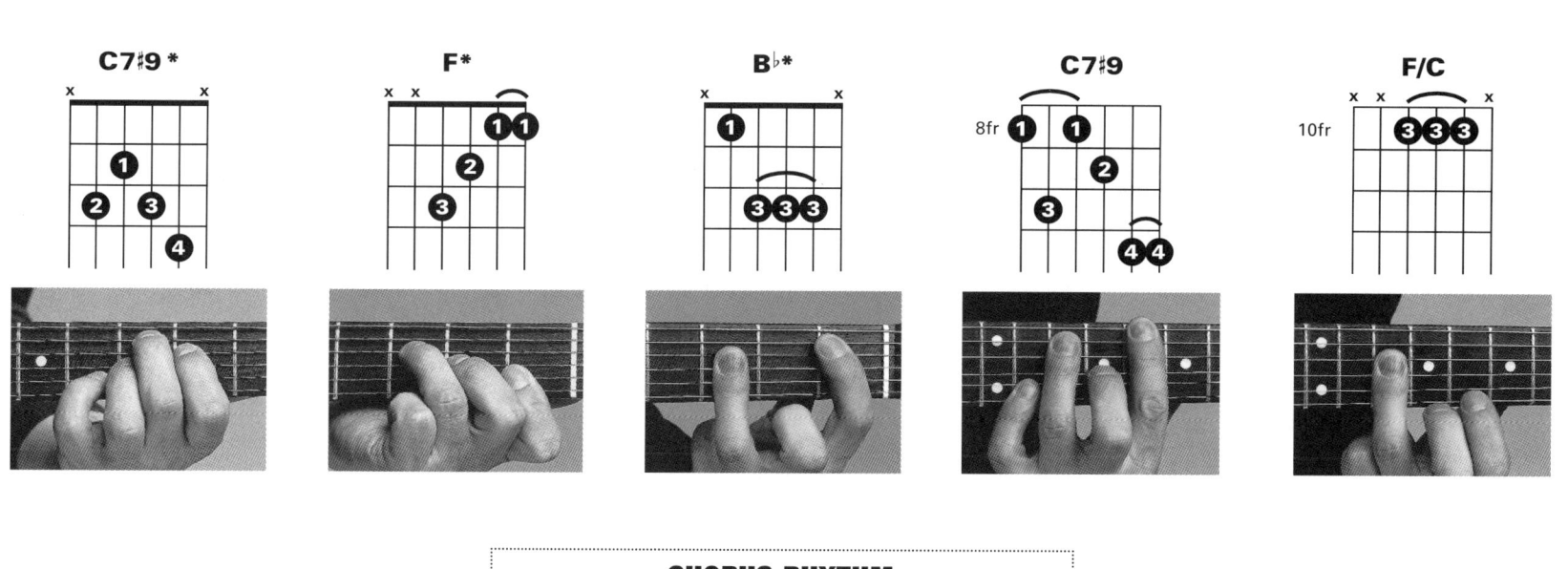

CHORUS RHYTHM
The rhythm in the chorus is very percussive, with accents on the 2nd and 4th beats.

Intro

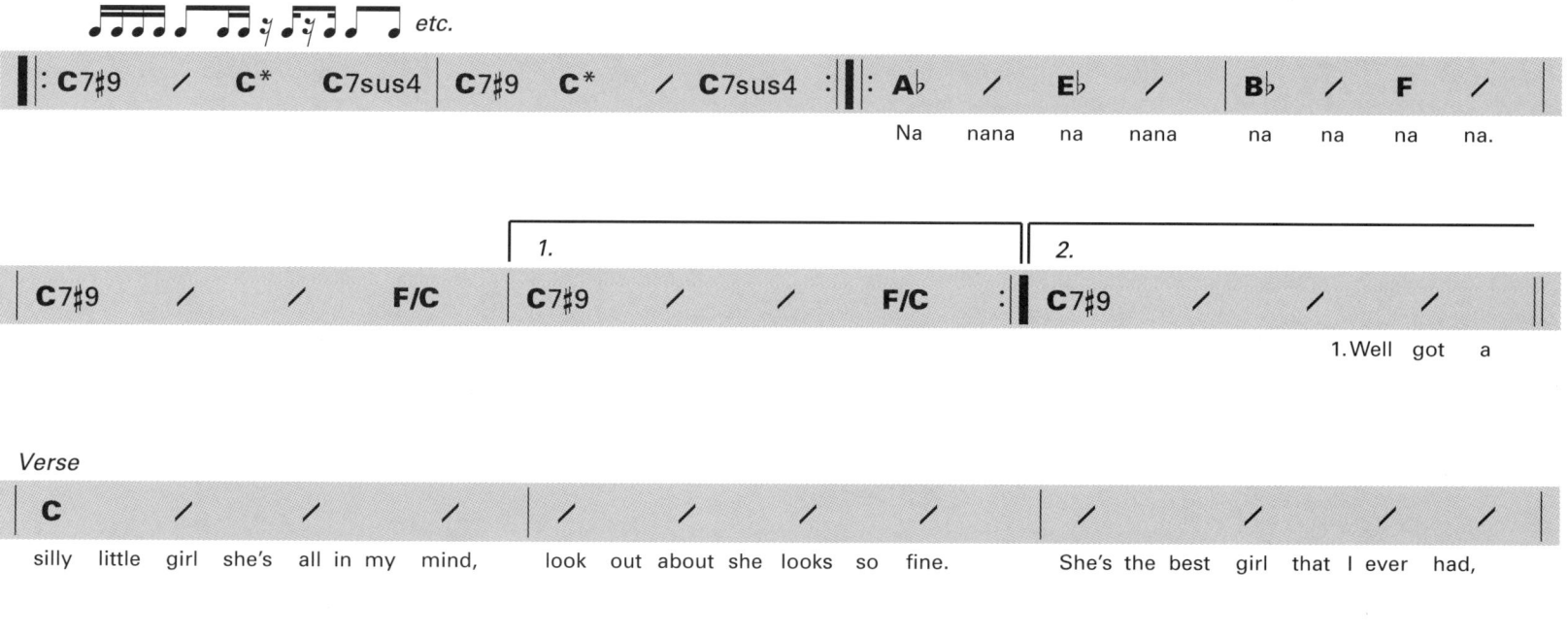

Na nana na nana na na na na.

1. Well got a

Verse

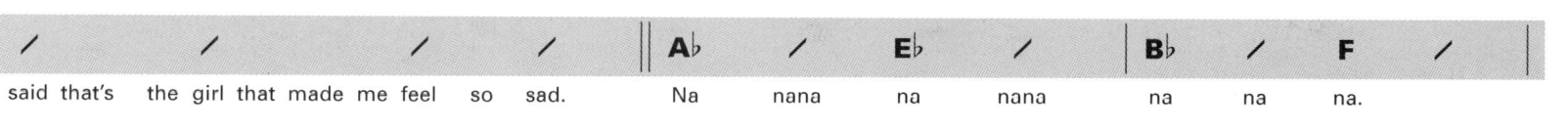

silly little girl she's all in my mind, look out about she looks so fine. She's the best girl that I ever had,

said that's the girl that made me feel so sad. Na nana na nana na na na.

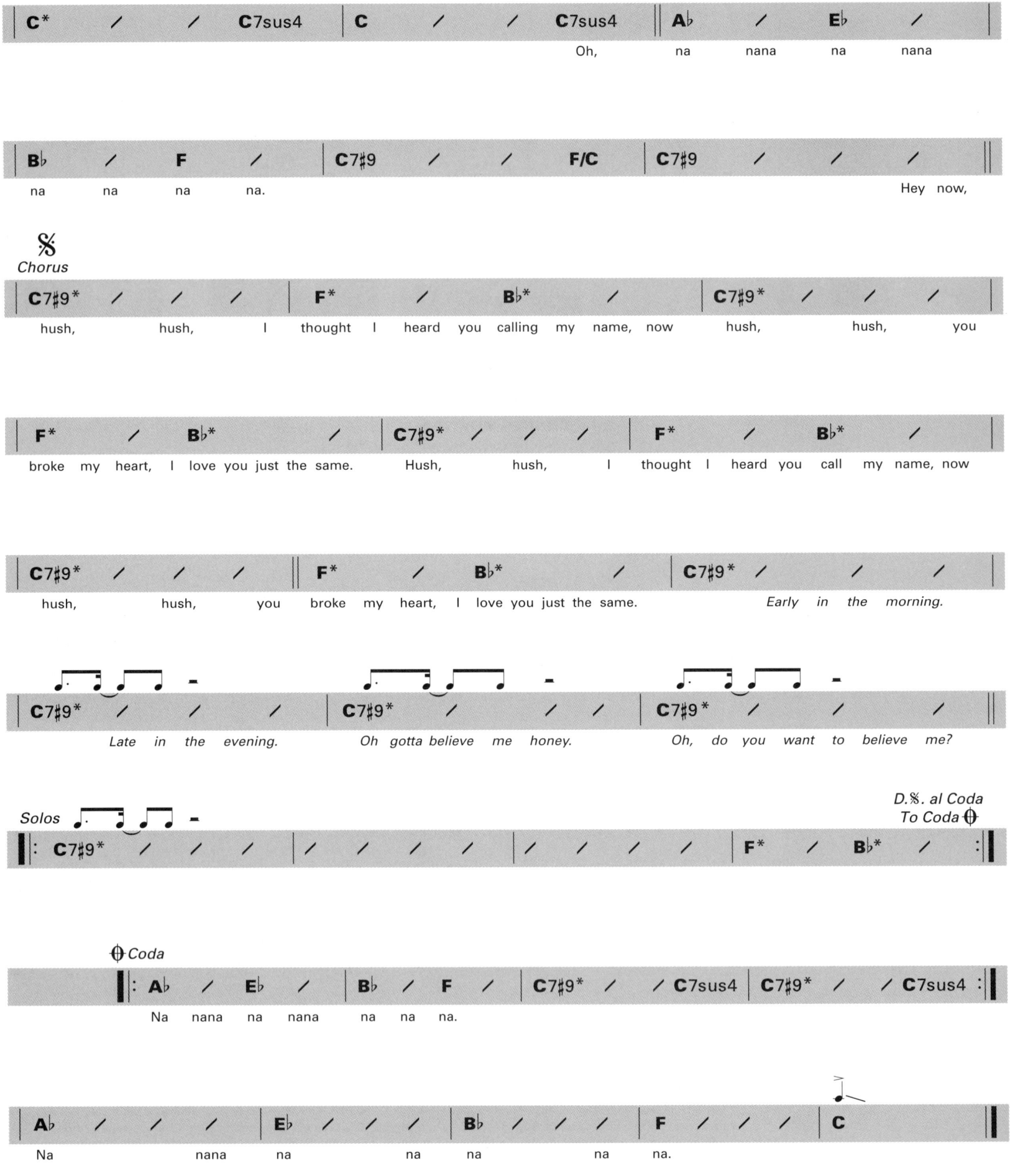

Words & Music by Joe South.
© Copyright 1967 Lowery Music Company Incorporated, USA.
BMG Music Publishing Limited, 69-79 Fulham High Street, London SW6. This arrangement © Copyright 2000 BMG Music Publishing Limited.
All Rights Reserved. International Copyright Secured.

I Can See For Miles

Pedal Notes In The Bass

CHORD CHECK

See *Chord Chemistry* page 38.

On its release in 1967, Pete Townshend considered this to be the ultimate Who record. John Entwistle's driving bass plays the pedal notes throughout the verses and choruses, punctuated by Pete's powerful guitar (not to mention Keith Moon's unique drumming!). Besides playing the power chords, the guitar can play the **E** pedal. Here's the two bar pattern for the intro and verse – watch out for the key change where the open **A** is pedalled.

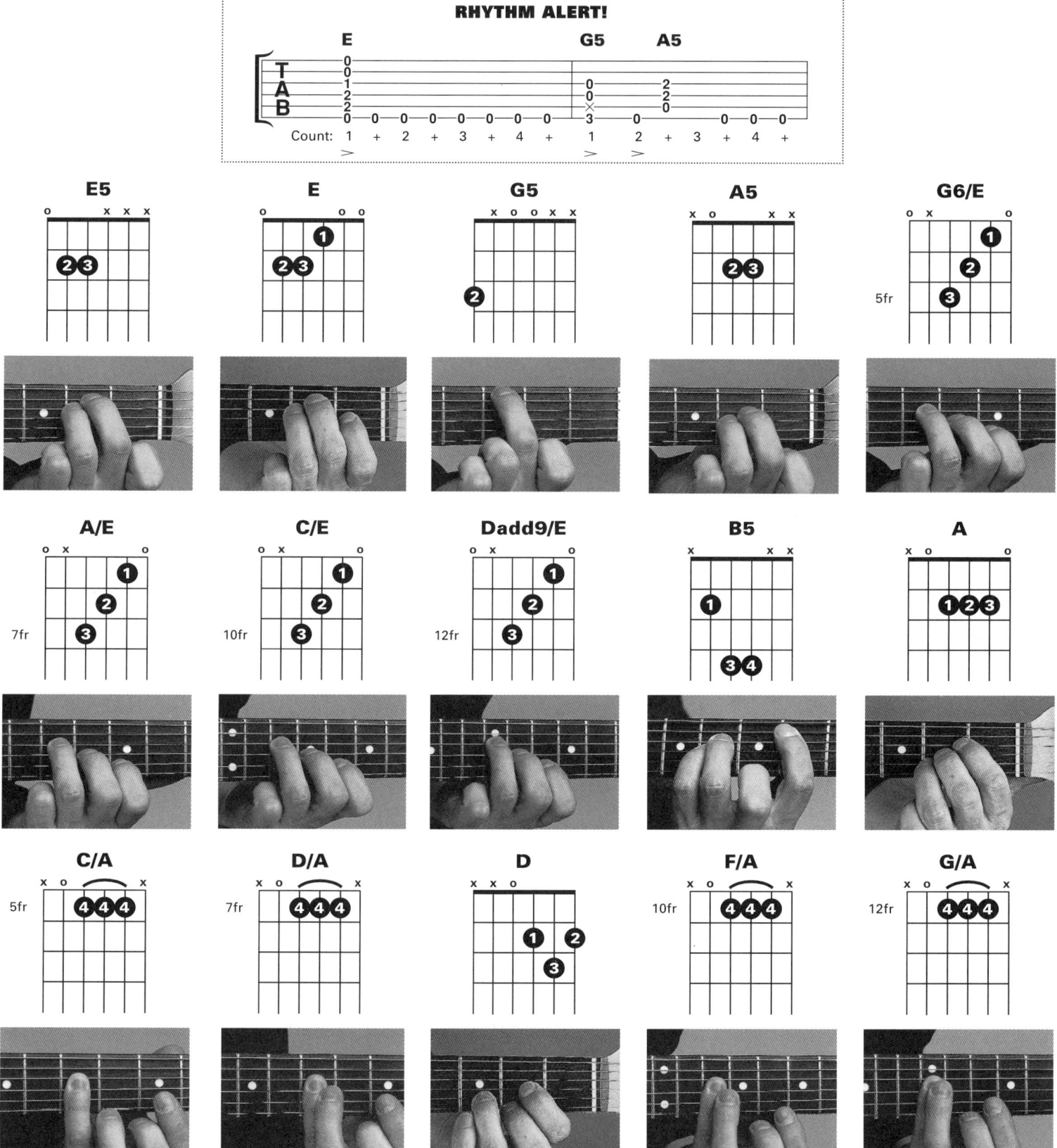

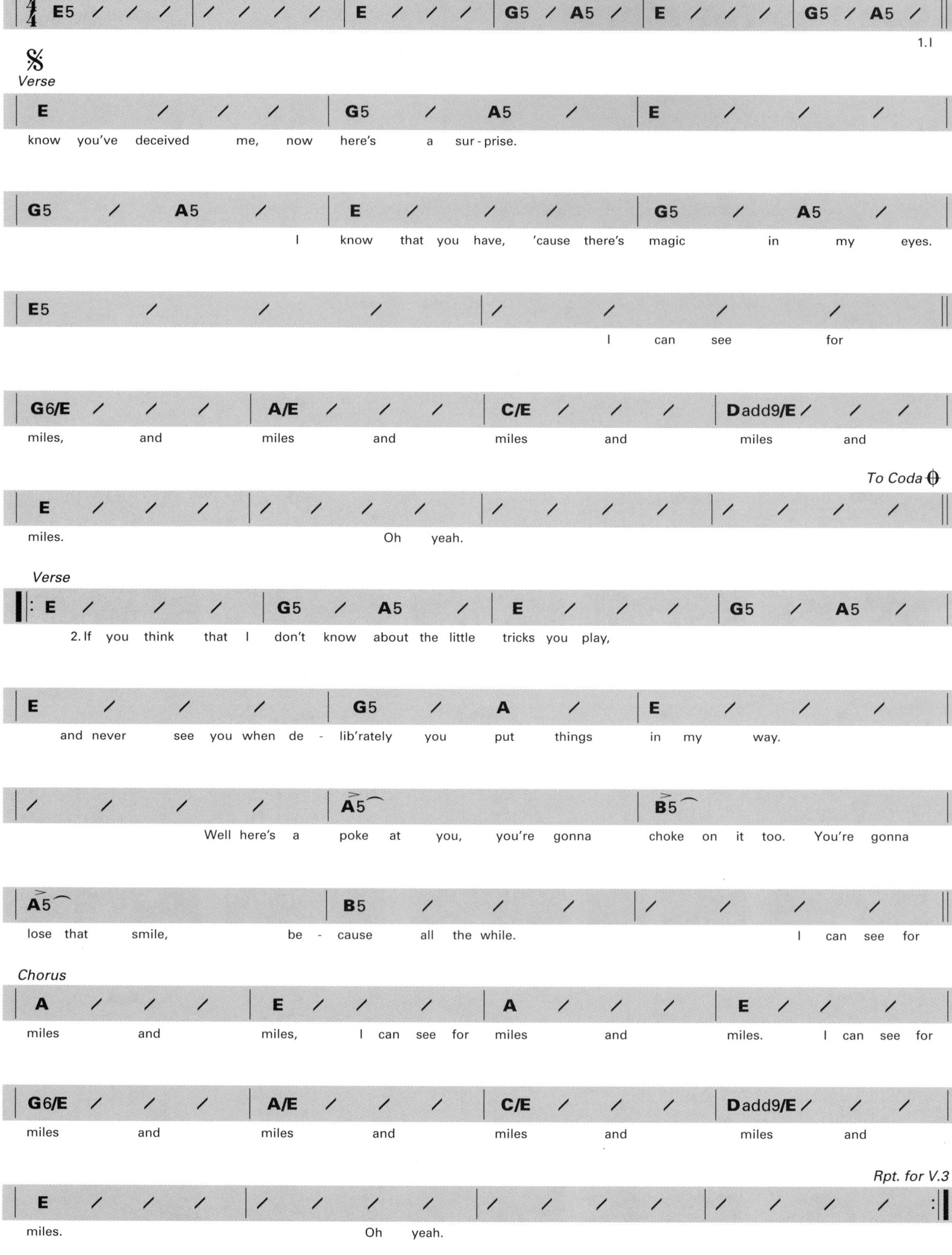

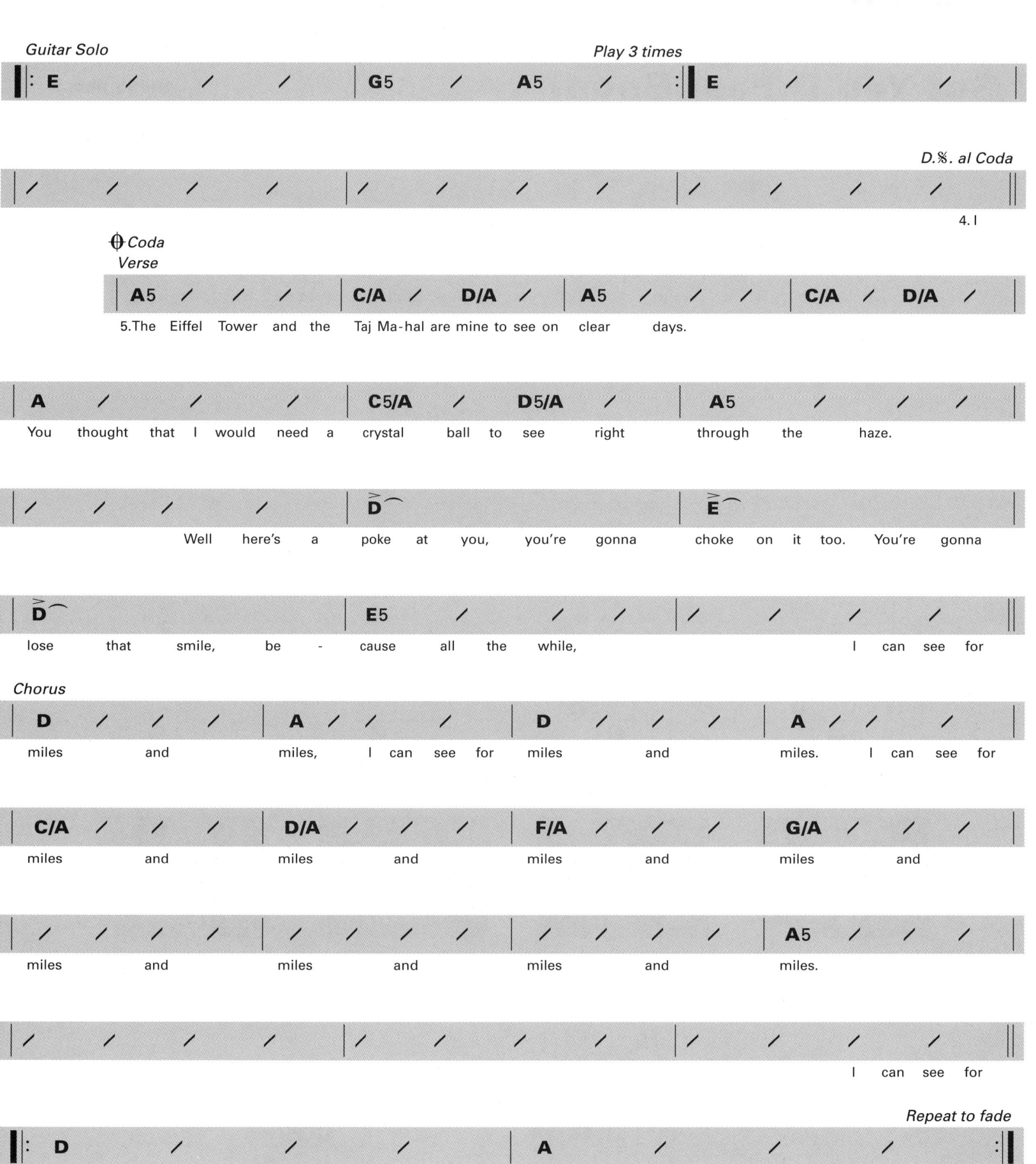

VERSE 3

You took advantage of my trust in you when I was so far away
I saw you holding lots of other guys and now you've got the nerve to say
That you still want me, well that's as may be
But you gotta stand trial because all the while...
I can see for miles... etc

Words & Music by Pete Townshend
© Copyright 1967 Fabulous Music Limited, Suite 2.07, Plaza 535 King's Road, London SW10.
All Rights Reserved. International Copyright Secured.

I Got You (I Feel Good)

Exploring Partial Chords

> **CHORD CHECK**
>
> See *Chord Chemistry*
> page 50.

James Brown and his band laid down the funkiest of tracks with Jimmy Nolen playing the crucial guitar part. Besides the unique voicings, he plays the chords on beat two of every other bar, so as not to interfere with the horns, and avoiding the usual 'two' and 'four' backbeat pattern. By bars 9 and 10 he joins the horns, playing stopped chords on beats 2 and 3, before joining the entire band with the 5 note crushing unison break in bars 11 and 12.

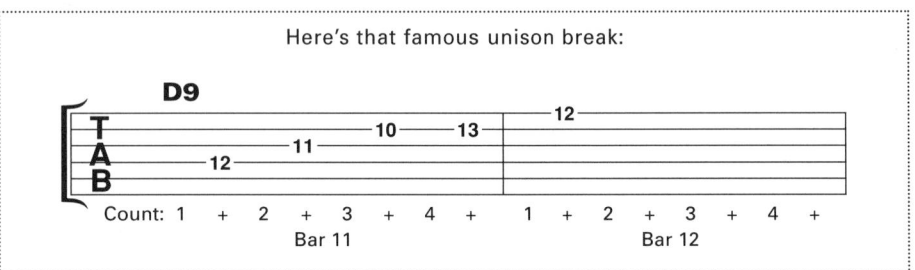

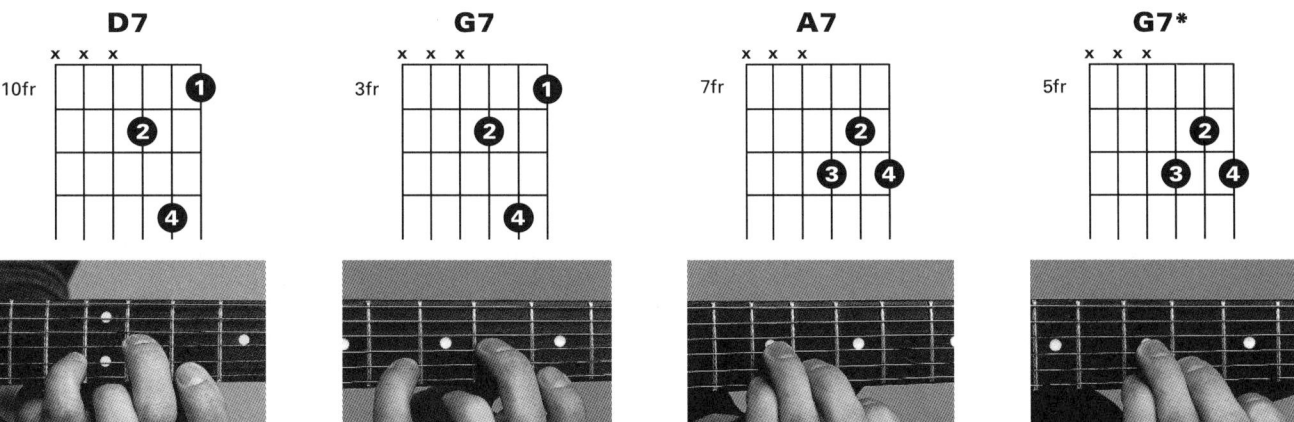

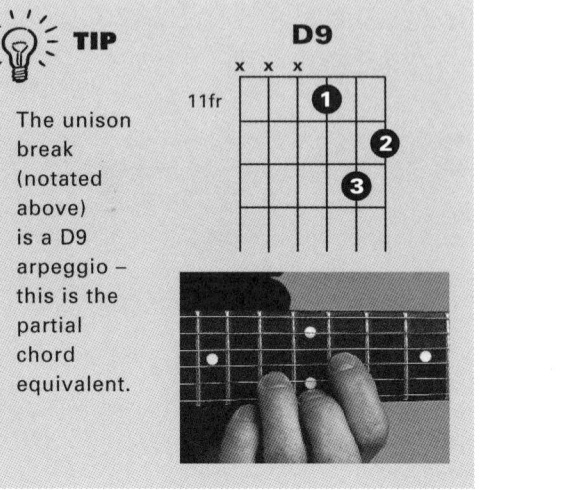

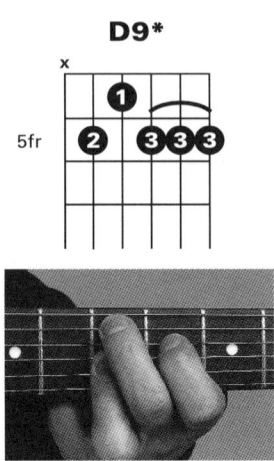

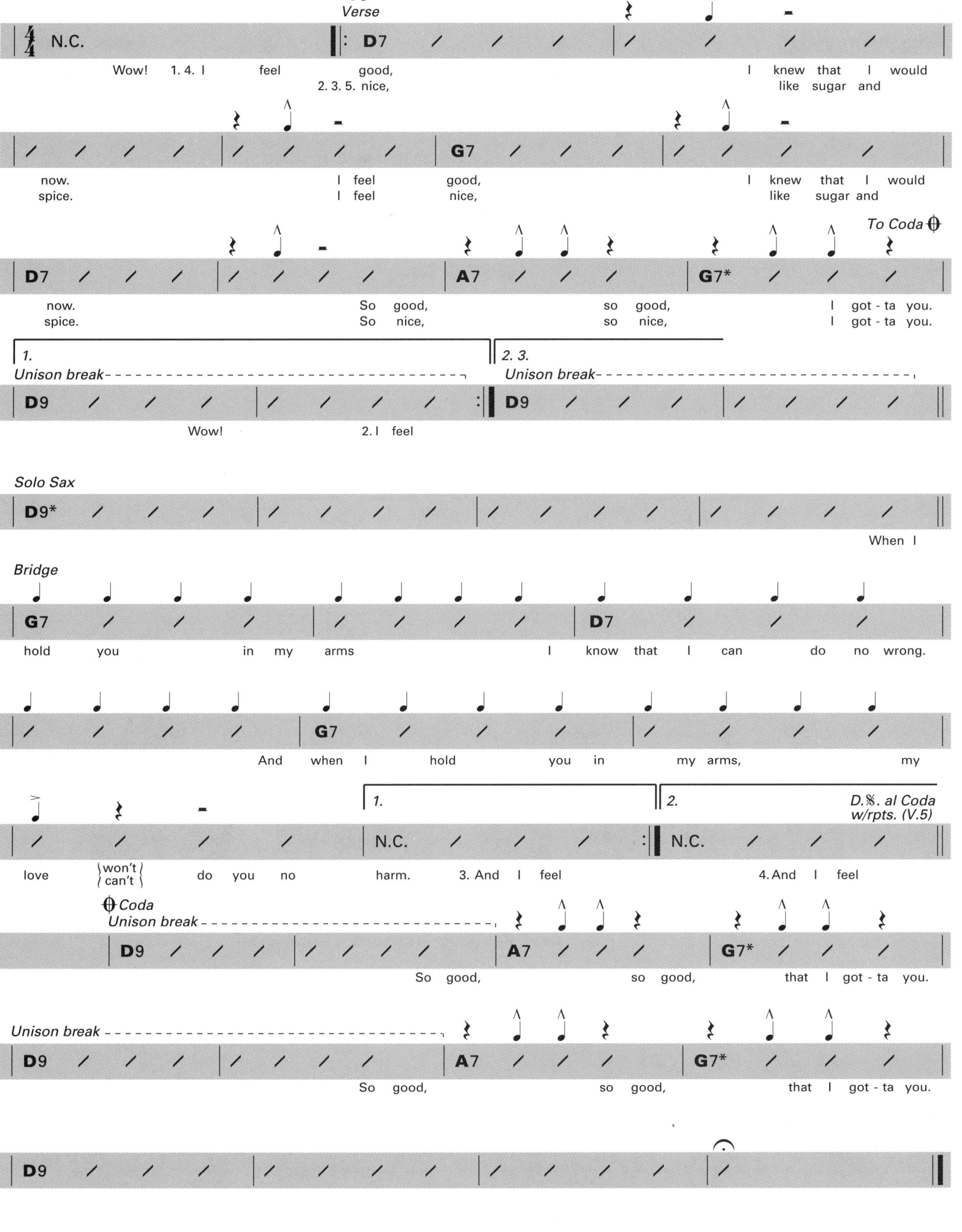

Words & Music by James Brown
© Copyright 1966 Fort Knox Music Company Incorporated, USA.
Lark Music Limited (Carlin), Iron Bridge House, 3 Bridge Approach, London NW1.
All Rights Reserved. International Copyright Secured.

Paranoid

Power Up!

> **CHORD CHECK**
>
> See *Chord Chemistry*
> page 50 & 51.

Crank up your amp and get your head down for this Black Sabbath classic. Tony Iommi plays most of the power chords with the root on the 6th string for that heavy rock sound, with the **E5** chord played at the 12th fret. Try lightly muting the strings with your right hand while playing this most famous of riffs:

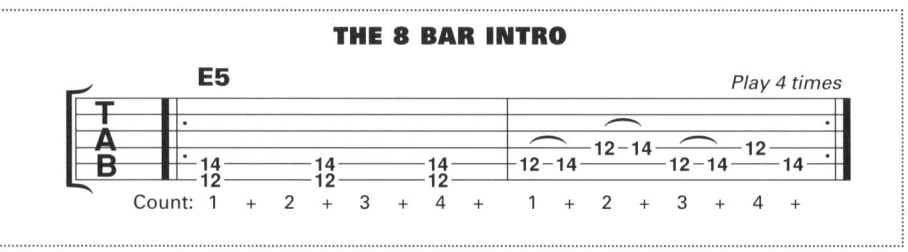

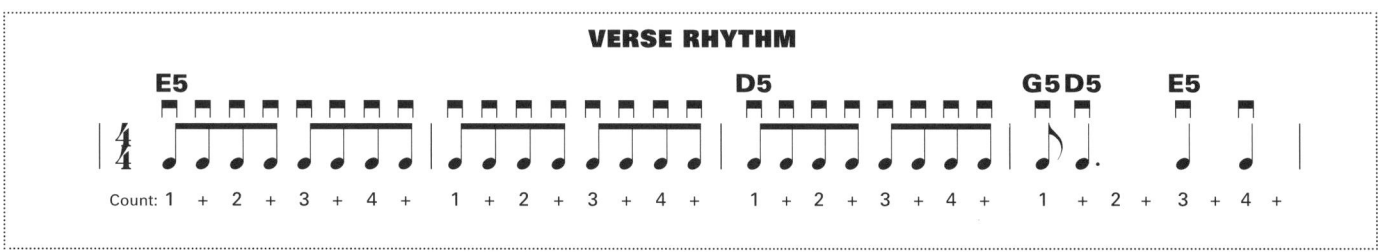

Throughout the chorus play big held power chords and think of Wembley!

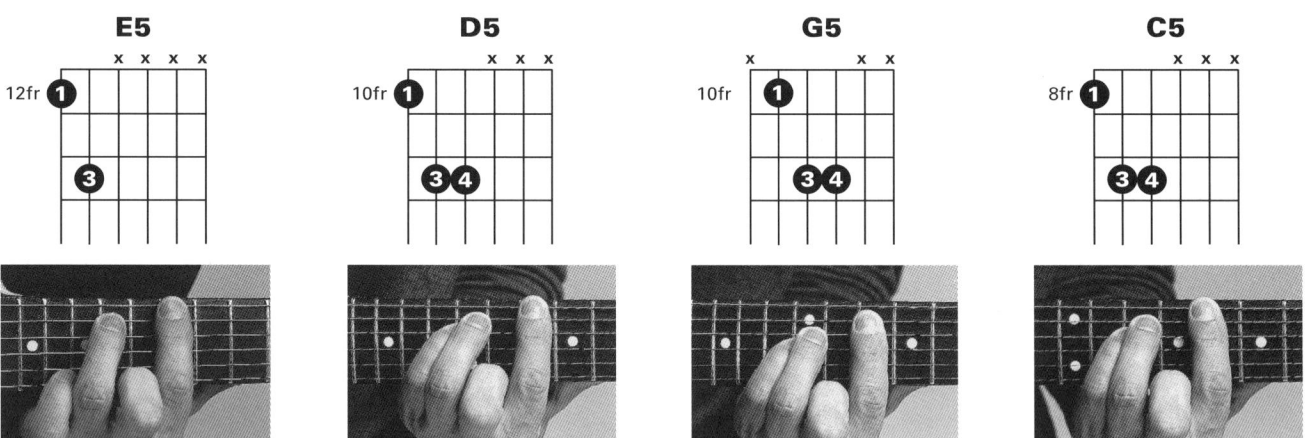

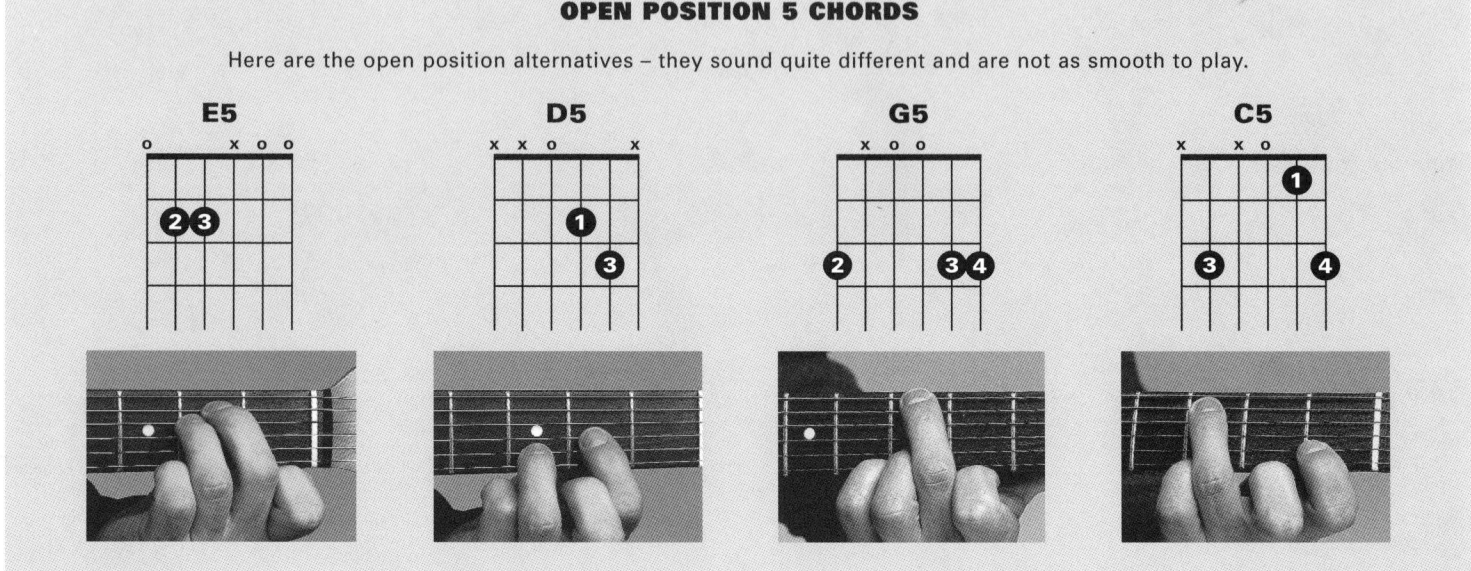

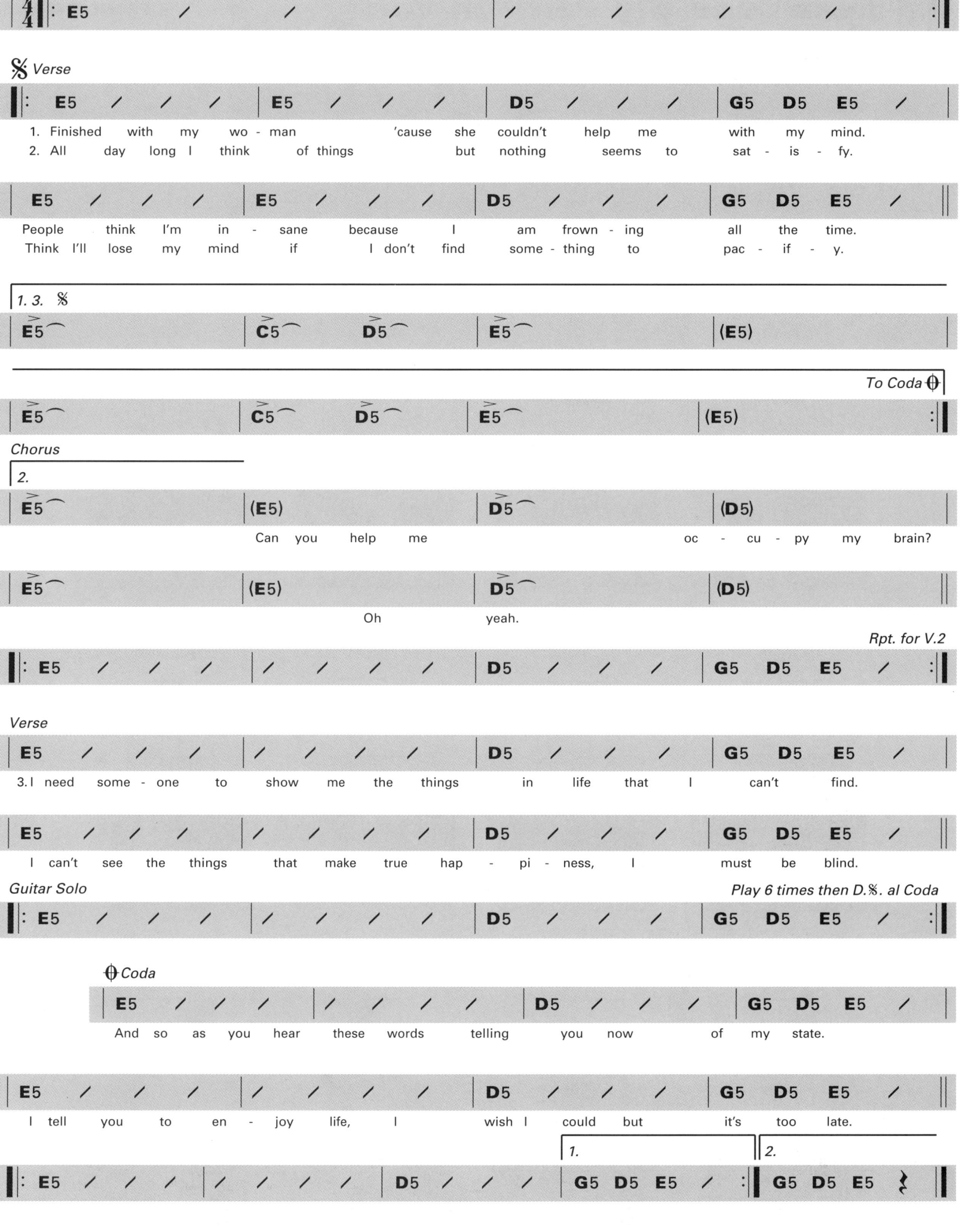

Words & Music by Terence Butler, John Osbourne, Frank Iommi & William Ward
© Copyright 1970 Westminster Music Limited, Suite 2.07, Plaza 535 King's Road, London SW10.
All Rights Reserved. International Copyright Secured.

If I Ever Lose My Faith In You

The Grand Finale.

> **CHORD CHECK**
>
> See *Chord Chemistry*
> page 56.

Test your knowledge with Sting's award winning anthem from his *Ten Summoners Tales* album. You'll find that this song has probably the biggest variation of chords you've come across - so it's a perfect one to finish on. You'll be using many very specific chord voicings, so pay close attention to the chord boxes. Also, be careful to mute the top string where indicated - a ringing E could suggest a completely different chord.

So here's your chance to play all those chords you learnt in *Chord Chemistry*, in one song.

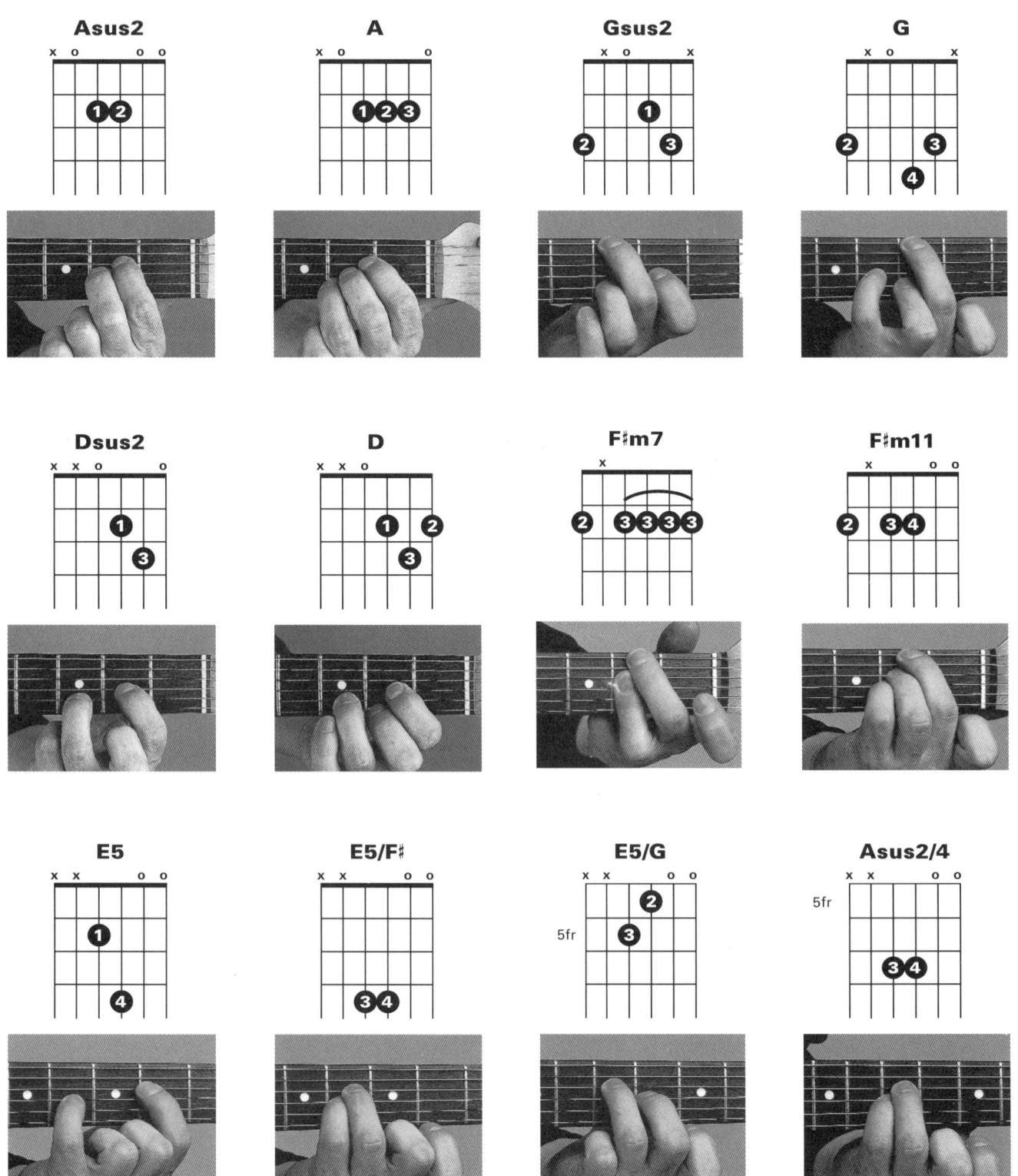

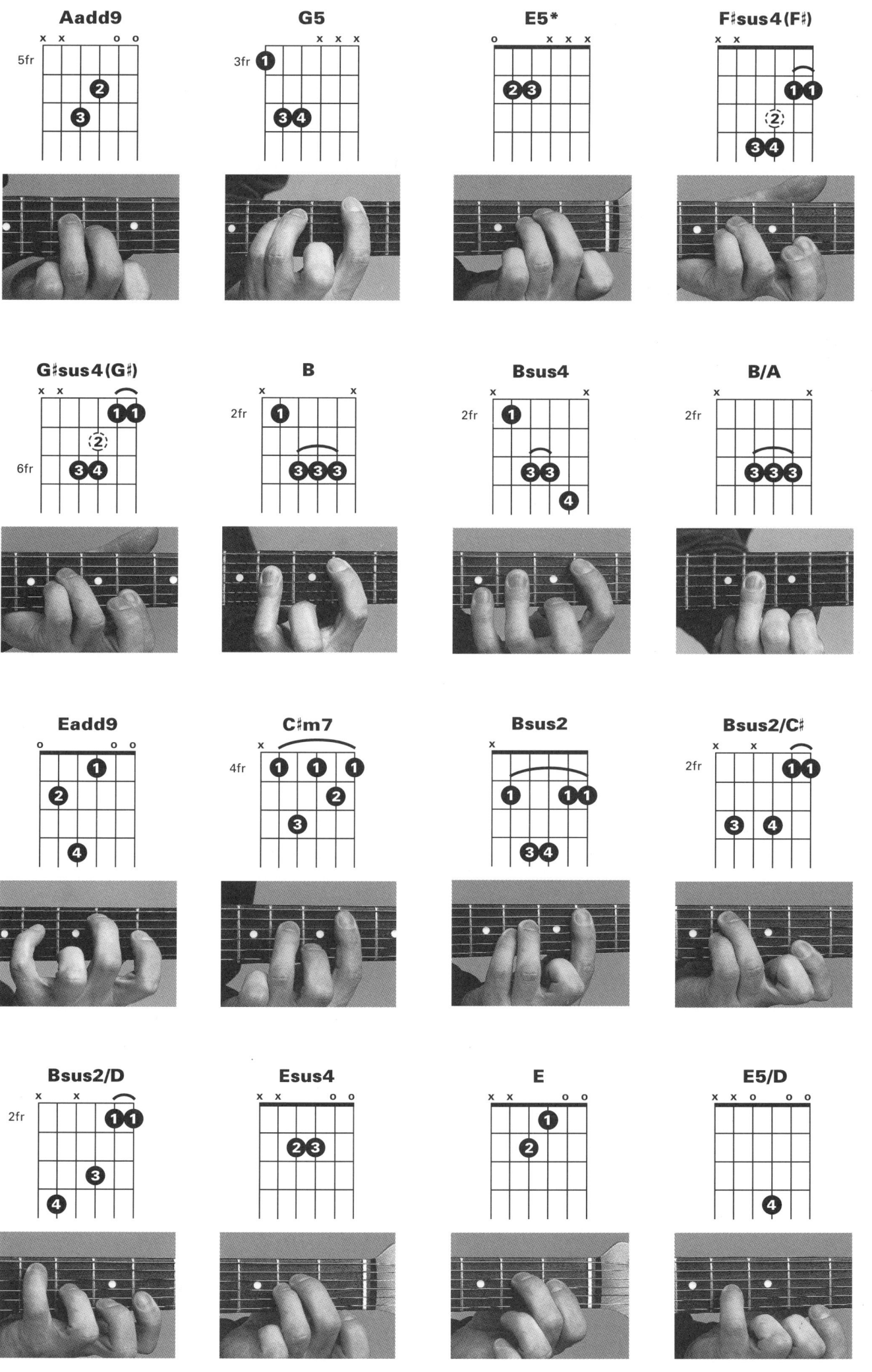

Verse

| $\frac{4}{4}$ ‖: **A**sus2 ╱ **A** ╱ | **G**sus2 ╱ **G** ╱ | **D**sus2 ╱ **D** ╱ |

1. You could say I lost my faith in sci - ence and pro - gress.

| **D**sus2 ╱ **D** ╱ | **A**sus2 ╱ **A** ╱ | **G**sus2 ╱ **G** ╱ |

You could say I lost my belief in the holy church.

| **D**sus2 ╱ **D** ╱ | **D**sus2 ╱ **D** ╱ | **A**sus2 ╱ **A** ╱ |

You could say I

| **G**sus2 ╱ **G** ╱ | **D**sus2 ╱ **D** ╱ | **D**sus2 ╱ **D** ╱ |

lost my sense of direction.

To Coda ⊕

| **A**sus2 ╱ **A** ╱ | **F♯m7** ╱ **F♯m7** ╱ ‖

Yes, you could say all of this and worse but...

Chorus

| **E**5 ╱ ╱ ╱ | **E**5/**F♯** ╱ ╱ ╱ | **E**5/**G** ╱ ╱ ╱ |

If I ever lose my faith in you,

| **A**sus2/4 ╱ **A**add9 ╱ | **E**5 ╱ ╱ ╱ | **E**5/**F♯** ╱ ╱ ╱ |

there'd be nothing left for me to do.

Play 2°only - ⌐   *Repeat for V.2*

| **E**5/**G** ╱ ╱ ╱ | **A**sus2/4 ╱ **A**add9 ╱ | **A**sus2/4 ╱ **A**add9 ╱ ‖

Interlude

| **G**5 ╱ **E**5* ╱ | **G**5 ╱ **E**5* ╱ | **G**5 ╱ **E**5* ╱ | **G**5 ╱ **E**5* ╱ ‖

Bridge

| **F♯**sus4 ╱ ╱ ╱ | **G♯**sus4 ╱ ╱ ╱ | **A**add9 ╱ ╱ ╱ |

I could be lost in - side their lies, with -

VERSE 2

Some would say I was a lost man in a lost world
You could say I lost my faith in the people on T.V.
You can say I lost my belief in the politicians
They all seem like game show hosts to me.

VERSE 3

Never saw no miracle of science
That didn't go from a blessing to a curse
Never saw no military solution
That didn't end up as something worse but...

Words & Music by Sting. © Copyright 1993 G.M. Sumner & Steerpike Limited.
EMI Music Publishing Limited/Magnetic Publishing Limited.
All Rights Reserved. International Copyright Secured.

Further Reading

Chord Chemistry
AM942580

We've all watched someone play and wondered "What's that chord? It sounds great!". **Chord Chemistry** shows you how to create those great-sounding chords and chord sequences.

Right from the start you'll find out how to spice up basic repertoire, creating, for example, 'add' and 'sus' chords. You'll also learn 7ths and 9ths, and how to mix slash, root, pedal and barre chords into your sequences. Throughout, you'll be able to play along with the accompanying CD.

The **Chord Chemistry** system is the exciting new way to transform your basic chord skills into professional-sounding guitar parts!

It's Easy To Bluff...

Be an instant expert with this great new series from Music Sales. Each book includes player/band biographies, a history of the guitar style, musical examples, and lots of handy tips and tricks to help you 'bluff your way through' any situation!

Blues Guitar
AM955196

Rock Guitar
AM955218

Metal Guitar
AM955207

Jazz Guitar
AM955185

Music Theory
AM958585

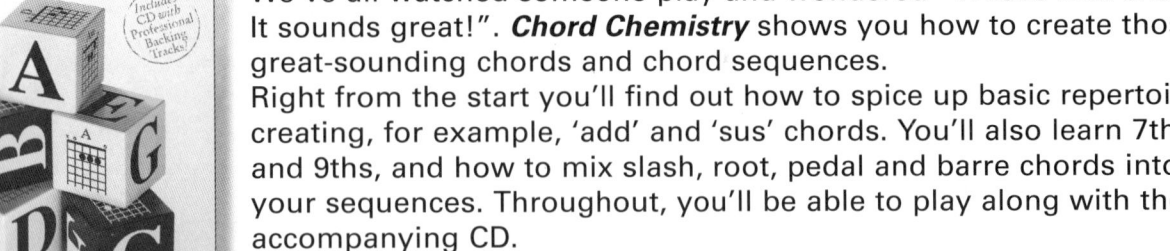

Guitar... To Go!

This handy little series focuses on four specific techniques, to allow you to 'short-cut' to what you want to know.

Guitar Scales... To Go!
AM954261

Guitar Riffs... To Go!
AM954250

Guitar Chords... To Go!
AM954240

Guitar Tunings... To Go!
AM954272

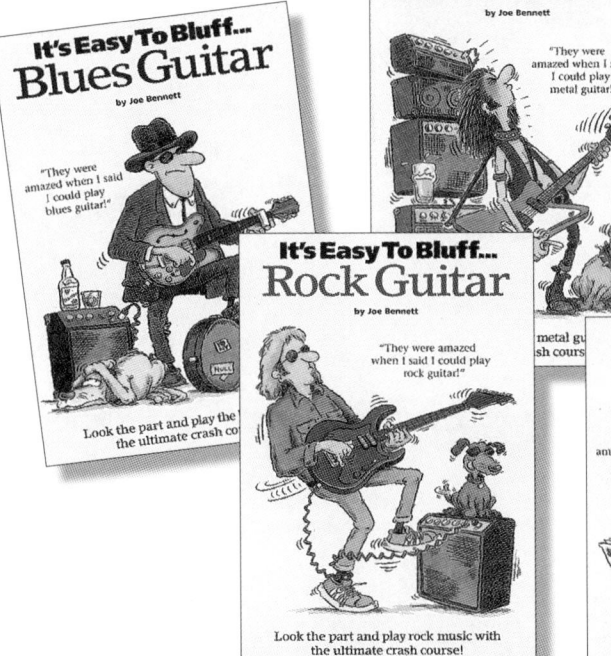

48 CHORD CHEMISTRY SONGBOOK